PRAISE FOR GO BIG

These guys don't just think big—they live and minister big! I love their passion, creativity, and enthusiasm. But most of all, I love that they are using their platform for a cause bigger than themselves.
> **CRAIG GROESCHEL** Author of *WEIRD: Because Normal Isn't Working*

God built us not so we can achieve mediocrity, but so we can achieve extraordinary outcomes. Go Big gives a simple yet powerful path to achieve the extraordinary.
> **STEVEN K. SCOTT** Author of *The Richest Man Who Ever Lived: King Solomon's Secrets to Success, Wealth, and Happiness*

Having a Go Big mind-set isn't an option. It's the only option. Go Big every day!
> **TAMMY KLING** Coauthor of *The Compass*, Founder of Write it Out

Whether your dream is to start a business or star in the NBA, a Go Big mind-set is key.
> **TYREKE EVANS** 2010 NBA Rookie of the Year, Sacramento Kings

MAKE YOUR SHOT COUNT

IN THE CONNECTED WORLD

GO BIG

CORY COTTON

TYNDALE HOUSE PUBLISHERS, INC., CAROL STREAM, ILLINOIS

Visit Tyndale online at www.tyndale.com.

TYNDALE and Tyndale's quill logo are registered trademarks of Tyndale House Publishers, Inc.

Go Big: Make Your Shot Count in the Connected World

Designed by Dean H. Renninger

Edited by Jonathan Schindler

Published in association with the literary agency of Roger Gibson, 2085 Lakeshore Drive, Branson, MO 65616.

Library of Congress Cataloging-in-Publication Data

Cotton, Cory.
  Go Big : make your shot count in the connected world / by Cory Cotton.
    p. cm.
  Includes bibliographical references.
  ISBN 978-1-4143-6137-6 (hc)
  1. Basketball. 2. Video games and children. 3. YouTube (Electronic resource)
4. Basketball players—Conduct of life. I. Title.
  GV885.C626 2011
  796.323—dc23   2011020887

Printed in the United States of America

20 19 18 17 16
8   7   6   5   4

To that moment in your life when you finally decide
to do that thing you know you should be doing.
That moment is now.

✦　✦　✦

TABLE OF CONTENTS

INTRODUCTION
MAKING YOUR SHOT COUNT

The door slowly opened, and as the bright light poured over us, a booming loudspeaker filled the Los Angeles air:

Please join me in welcoming to the ESPYs the Internet sensation, the premier trick basketball shooting entertainers, Dude Perfect!

As applause took over, it would have been natural to survey the crowd. But at that moment, all I could do was watch my brown Texas boots take their first ever steps on a long red carpet.

It would have been impossible to guess almost two years before, when my five college roommates and I started shooting and filming crazy basketball shots in our backyard, that this was what we'd have to look forward to. We were just ordinary guys with a passion for competition and a basketball hoop. We still went to classes, still hung out with our friends, and still faced the same difficulties that every other college student faces. But after we launched a YouTube video of some of our favorite shots, we were thrilled to see it rapidly gain momentum—so

GO BIG TIP

If you don't act quickly and wisely to stand out in the crowd, an idea marked with your fingerprint could easily end up with someone else's name on the package.

much momentum, in fact, that it wound up on *Good Morning America* only two days later. At that point, we realized we'd stumbled into a niche in the YouTube world.

Now, two years and more than forty-five million views later, so much has happened that it would take two books this size to explain it all. But as I look back on our journey so far, I realize that from day one, our motto has remained the same: "go big." This phrase—our overall mind-set—has been the filter through which we've run all our decisions, and it has truly shaped us into who we are.

But before you read any further, I want you to know exactly what you're getting into. The book you're holding is for people who want to go big . . . period. Some people are okay with mediocre. Some people are okay with floating through life. We are not those people. This book is for those who want to pursue excellence, who want to blow it out of the water and chase down their dreams. This book is for those who want to go big—and who refuse to apologize for it.

Our faces may be on the cover, but this book isn't about us; it's about you. Our hope is that as we explain our Go Big approach to life, you will establish the same mind-set and experience the blessing of seeing your most heartfelt dream become a reality.

Do this for me: Compare that dream to one of our trick basketball shots. You could envision it all day, plan it out, and even imagine what it would feel like to make it, but in order to experience it, you have to actually take the shot. Sometimes you miss; sometimes you miss *badly*; sometimes you even break the backboard. But after however many tries it takes, the cool-

est thing can happen: you make it. And when you do, there's nothing in the world quite like it.

Unfortunately, few people take their shot. Sometimes that's because they don't know what dream to aim for. More often, though, it's because of fears and obstacles that seem impossible to overcome.

Then, of those who do take their shot, even fewer make it count. Taking your shot is the first step, but making it count is the key. And while making it count is the most critical part, it can also be the most difficult. Why is that? Simply put, the rules have changed. The world that required an adult to work fifteen years to build a business—a brand—is disappearing fast. Today, a real-deal, moneymaking brand can emerge overnight, almost instantly. In this new, connected world, making your shot count requires taking full advantage of the resources this connected world offers.

The good news is that we're here to help. We've just spent two years taking risks, pushing limits, seeking advice, and writing it all down—for you. Now I get to share with you all the exciting things we've learned about leveraging the opportunities of this new, connected world.

From the backyard to the front page, we've created a sustainable business from shooting crazy basketball shots. We've worked with NBA players, filmed internationally broadcasted television commercials, and leveraged our platform to help others. We've experienced the blessing of discovering, chasing, and achieving a dream. Bottom line: we want that for you. We believe there is a purpose for your life, and part of it is to fulfill your dream. Obviously we can't force you to pursue your

MEET THE DUDES

Cory 100% Cotton

Go Big Moment: Dude Perfect winning the Texas A&M dodgeball championship

Go Big Dream: Dunk from the free-throw line. Or from the ground.

My Best Kept Secret: I'm bad at telling time on analog clocks. I was homeschooled for two years. Mom dropped the ball.

Favorite Shot: Ramp Shot. Sketchy, but awesome.

DudePerfect.com

THE FIVE PRINCIPLES

GET EXCITED

+ + +

OWN IT

+ + +

BLINK LATER

+ + +

INSPIRE OTHERS

+ + +

GIVE BACK

dream—that's your decision—but by the end of this book, we'll ensure that you know how.

Throughout this book, we'll explore the five things you need to do in order to go big in the connected world. We'll look at how these five principles played out in Dude Perfect's story, and we'll explore the ways they can play out in yours.

First, we'll show you how to take your unique passions and strengths and turn them into a profession. Just imagine it—you could actually **Get Excited** about what you do. This is critical for one simple reason: if you don't love your work, neither will anyone else.

Next, we'll teach you how to formulate an effective business plan and show you how to bring your dream to reality. We'll empower you to fully embrace and relentlessly pursue your vision. We'll teach you how to **Own It**.

Time is often your greatest enemy. From everything we've seen, you need to act now or someone else will. We'll train you in the art of lightning-quick decision making and equip you to make the best use of the most precious resource you have. In this increasingly fast-moving, technological world, your window of opportunity is too short to blink. Because of this, do what we do: **Blink Later**.

Whatever your dream may be, establishing and gaining momentum through your efforts is essential to your success. We've discovered that the most powerful way to create lasting momentum is to **Inspire Others**. We'll explain how to uncover existing inspiration, create more from scratch, and transform every bit of it into lasting momentum.

Finally, we'll discuss leveraging your platform for a cause greater than yourself. Your opportunity to pursue a dream is a privilege—one you should be thankful for. We'll explore the concept of taking what you've been uniquely given and using that to benefit others in a powerful way. Both from a personal and a corporate viewpoint, it's important to shift our perspective from inward to outward, to **Give Back**.

In our college backyard only two short years ago, my five buddies and I made a shift from living a normal life to living a Go Big one. We're solid proof that in today's connected world, a lot can happen in a very short time. Even before we realized it, we followed these five principles. And if you'll do the same, it won't matter what age you are, where you're from, or how much money you have; it won't matter what you've been told or what you've told yourself; you can live your dream. That's right, you—not someone else—*you*. You *can* make your shot count in the connected world. You *can* go big. If you're ready, just turn the page.

PART ONE

GET EXCITED

CHAPTER 1
HOW IT ALL BEGAN

I got home from class about 2:00 p.m., and the guys were in the backyard playing basketball, or so I thought. I laughed as I heard Tyler shouting victoriously, "Boom!" I walked through the empty house, out the sliding door, and into the backyard. As it turned out, I wasn't the only one laughing. Sean, too, was almost in tears as Tyler strutted up to and around me, passionately reliving what I'd missed only moments before.

See, Ty does this ridiculous thing where he makes one-sided bets like, "If I throw this pocket knife into that tree all the way across our yard, you owe me twenty bucks." It's an obviously-there's-no-way-I-can-do-this kind of bet because if he misses, he doesn't owe the other person a dime. I realize I could have done a million different things with that twenty-dollar bill, but it ended up in Ty's wallet instead. Why we let him do this I don't know, except that the stuff he says always sounds so ridiculous.

MEET THE DUDES

Garrett Hilbert

Go Big Moment:
Walking the red carpet and meeting Dr. J

Go Big Dream:
Doing trick shots with Rob Dyrdek at his Fantasy Factory

My Best Kept Secret:
I became my high school team's shooting guard after being banned from shooting three-pointers the year before.

Favorite Shot: Fishing Pole Shot

DudePerfect.com

All that to say, this was another one of those sucker moments, and Garrett, like we all have, fell into Tyler's clever trap.

Slapping the basketball repeatedly as he spoke, Ty built up anticipation. "Jimmy John's sandwich. Twenty-yard hook shot. Opposite side of the yard." Garrett couldn't resist. "Deal."

Ty swished it, earned a free lunch, and shared a resounding "boom!" with the once peaceful neighborhood. *That* was the hilarious celebration I'd walked in on. As we laughed in the backyard that sunny afternoon, we had no idea that the next couple of hours would change our lives forever.

But before we go there, I want you to think about something. For us—for Dude Perfect—our journey began in the fun of this one moment. When Tyler made that shot, an abnormal level of excitement welled up in us, and we noticed it. I'm not talking about some magical moment; I'm talking about a simple "ha ha, that was awesome—like, *really awesome*" moment. Others might have smiled and moved on; it might not have struck them the same way. But to us, because of our love for basketball and competition, we thought it was really exciting. And as you'll soon see, the rest of our story—backyard, front page, red carpet, and all—has been a continuation of that initial excitement.

Now, having explained that, I want to ask you two simple but potentially life-changing questions:

- First, have you paid enough attention to the things that excite you? Have you taken notice of the moments that are awesome—like, *really awesome*?
- And second, what are those things? What is it that thrills you? What is it that's almost unnaturally exciting to you?

The reason these questions are so important is that your unique answers are exactly that: unique. Because of who you—and you alone—are, you're wired to be extra passionate about certain things.

Take a moment and think about what this might look like in your life. Maybe people give you a hard time about something you care a lot about, something that isn't nearly as fascinating to them as it is to you. Maybe it's something you used to be passionate about, but because of other responsibilities, you've had to shelve that dream for a little while. Maybe it's something you've never even told anyone else about; it's a closet dream, something you assume others wouldn't understand, something you've kept hidden for a long time.

I've probably never met you, but let me tell you what I already know about you. I know you have an answer to those questions. And I know that, whatever your answer, you've thought a lot about that thing before. What I don't know is what you've done about it.

At some point or another, chances are you've wanted to take your unique passion to the next level. Maybe you've done that; maybe you haven't. But in order to measure that, we have to decide what exactly "the next level" is. In the end, that definition is up to you, but let me show you how it played out for us. After I finish this story, we'll offer you our suggestion, and I think you'll like the sound of it.

DUDE PERFECT: THE HOO-HA SHOT

DudePerfect.com

✦ ✦ ✦

Before I pulled into the driveway, Garrett, Tyler, and Sean had been shooting around in our grass backyard, breaking in the goal we'd purchased only a few days earlier. Turns out, without a place to dribble, all you can really do with a basketball goal is shoot on it.

As I laughed about the sandwich-winning story, Ty decided to prove it by shooting again from an even farther distance. Wanting to save the moment, Sean grabbed a camera. That, Sean, was a clutch idea. Changing it to video mode, Sean pressed the record button, and a couple of shots later, *swish*. Ty screamed, "Yes!" and threw down his hat in celebration. When we saw the shot on camera, it was obvious what we had to do next.

Camera rolling and competitive juices flowing, we tried to outdo each other. Standing on a rail. Backwards in a chair. Off the chimney. Over the fence. We'd shoot and show, shoot and show. It was a blast: some of the most competitive guys you could meet, a camera, and a basketball.

The defining moment came when Ty stepped up to a tree about thirty yards from the basket. A backwards over-the-header from that distance was ridiculous, and though Sean pointed the camera at him, I knew Ty was wasting our time. He'd already named a few of his shots for the camera, but this one was tougher to define. He simply said, "This shot doesn't even have a name." He let it fly, and with the ball in the air, he said, "Hoo-ha" . . . *swish*. Facing the opposite direction, Ty couldn't see it go in, but our reactions gave it away.

We all rushed toward Sean, dying to see the replay. We were impressed before we watched it again, but seeing it on camera turned out to be the drive for everything that followed. In real life, that shot had looked sweet; on camera, it looked fake. And that was a *very* good thing. Because Ty couldn't see it swish, his blank stare into the lens seemed to say, "No big deal." It looked hilarious. We didn't think anyone would believe it, but we wanted to know for sure. That was when we decided to make a video.

We kept making shots, but it was getting dark. So we soaked up all the time we could, called it a night, and went inside to check out the day's footage. We liked the shots we'd made, but we knew we didn't have enough to make a full video. We thought about other shots we could do the next day, and we smiled when Tyler said what all of us were thinking: "I want to go bigger." We wanted to shoot farther, more difficult shots. For round two, we wanted to go big.

Our classes ended at different times the next day, but we all came home as fast as we could. No one wanted to miss out on our new hobby. And, more important, no one wanted to be outdone. With camera charged, we went to the backyard and started recording. After a few mediocre land shots, our attention turned toward the roof of the house. We had bounced a few off of the roof, but we hadn't shot any *from* it yet. Unsurprisingly, Tyler was the first to scout it out, and with the camera's record light on, he invented what would turn out to be his favorite type of shot. Looking back over his shoulder, Tyler declared, "This is the laser shot." Like the former high school quarterback he is, Tyler took the ball in one hand and unleashed a rocket, sending a frozen rope through the net on his very first try.

TRICK SHOOTING 101

If you try a shot off your roof, consult your local authorities to make sure it's cool with them. Otherwise someone else will.

INSTANT REPLAY

Watching our footage is almost as much fun as filming it. We never know exactly how it's going to look until we see it on a bigger screen. So from the very beginning, crowding around our day's results has been one of our favorite parts of the process.

TRICK SHOOTING 101

When transporting your goal by truck, avoid low hanging branches as they can damage your goal, truck, and passengers.

As the day progressed and our creativity grew, we knew we'd have to move the goal off-site to go even bigger. We headed to a nearby park and unloaded. To say the least, we caused some comical confusion as we rolled our goal past the people playing on the park's outdoor basketball court. *Excuse us, fellas; we brought our own.* After making some sweet shots there, we only needed one more shot to finish our video—a really far one. Distance-wise, we hadn't pulled off anything too impressive yet, so we set our sights on something big.

On our way home, we passed a friend's house, one with a front yard large enough to distance the house at least forty yards from the street. We'd found our big finish: forty yards from our friend's roof into the goal in the back of the truck. We rolled the camera for about ten minutes. It was windy that day, but with a little patience, Tyler nailed it. Somewhere in between excited and exhausted, we called it a wrap.

That night, as we crowded around the kitchen table and two days' worth of footage, a certain clip caught our attention. On day two, Sean and Tyler had filmed an introduction to begin our trick shot video. They'd set up two chairs in the backyard, and since they were the only ones there at the moment, Sean had set the camera on the rail of our deck. He pressed the record button, looked at the screen, and the view was exactly what he wanted. Pleased, he said, "Dude, perfect." We instantly loved it. Our name, our brand, and the phrase in all our videos was born.

We didn't set out to create a company, and we had absolutely no idea about the adventure ahead of us. What we did know was that we were doing something that excited us, something that stemmed from our love for competition. We knew we were having fun.

Now I promised you our suggestion to the "next level" question I asked earlier, and here it is. If you're not consistently getting excited about what you're doing, maybe you shouldn't be doing it. We're just college students, but already we've seen too many unenthusiastic answers to the question "What do you do for a living?" So here's a thought: if you don't have to fight back the urge to smile when you answer that question, you may need to reevaluate what you do.

Before you roll your eyes, let me explain. First of all, I realize that passion isn't everything, and not every passion is created equal. There are some passions that might be better if they remained hobbies. But while passion isn't *everything*, it is crucial. Passion is a good indicator of where your best efforts will be spent. We'll talk about this over the course of the next two chapters, but it's worth considering now: are you more likely to go big, to do the hard work necessary to achieve excellence, for something that excites you or for something that bores you? Getting excited puts you in a better position to take your shot and make it count. Passion may not be everything, but it's definitely worth your careful attention.

I also realize that not everyone is in a position to drop everything immediately and follow where their excitement leads. It's a lot easier for college guys with limited responsibilities to make trick basketball videos and travel promoting them. For someone working two jobs just to make ends meet, it's much harder to start chasing a dream. But thinking about what gets you excited is worth doing, whatever your next step is. When you know what it is that gets you excited, you'll be in a better position, now or in the future, to capitalize on the opportunities that come your way—or to create your own opportunities.

DUDE PERFECT: BACKYARD EDITION

DudePerfect.com

GO BIG TIP

Pay attention to your passions.

Discovering your passion is always the first step, whether you take what you're excited about to the next level immediately or somewhere down the line.

And getting excited isn't about the money. Why? Because this book isn't a get-rich-quick scheme. Do we legitimately believe that you *can* make money doing something you instinctively love? Yes. Have we? Yes. But for anyone who does something they love for a living, the smiling answer to the *what do you do* question almost never comes from the money; it comes from the job itself. We believe that everyone has something significant to offer, and doing something you love may be your best opportunity to offer it. So *that* is our suggestion. In the connected world we live in, we've been able to go big with a passion of ours. In the same way, we want to help you make your shot count and go big with what you love. Now if that feels unrealistic, you need to keep reading. And fast.

CHAPTER 2
WHAT WE REALLY DO BEST

Think about a huge, wildly successful company, a real global brand. Who comes to mind? For me, it's Apple, Inc. According to Interbrand—the world's leading brand consultantcy—Apple is the fastest-growing global brand, and for good reason. In almost every category, the company has set the bar for excellence. And while Apple's ingenuity, product quality, clarity of vision, and customer satisfaction are all examples of subjects the company is well qualified to teach, one category rises above the rest, both in appearance and in importance: passion.

Whether you're listening to Steve Jobs or one of his T-shirt-wearing Apple Store employees, you can't help but get the impression that everyone working for Apple loves what they do. From the top down, this incredible passion seeps out everywhere. It starts with Jobs, whose personal passion is responsible for almost everything Apple. It trickles down to the product design team that, with a remarkable determination for excellence, consistently creates some of the world's most life- and culture-altering products. It makes its way into television commercials that display competition-bashing levels of confidence. And as the money crosses the store counters, Jobs's passion—once confined to a dream of his own—turns countless doubters into passionate, Apple-loving, word-of-mouth salespeople.

Whether you find yourself in the Mac or PC camp, as you start your Go Big journey, it's crucial that you grab hold of this first principle: Get Excited. The reason behind this principle is simple: *passion positions excellence*. When you get excited about what you do, you're putting yourself in the best possible position for excellence. This is because those who are truly passionate about something have a higher potential for excellence—a stronger incentive to do the best they possibly can—than those without that built-in motivator. See, the power lies in the fact that true excitement can't be faked, not really.

Think back to your least favorite subject in school. You had a terrible time focusing because it bored you to tears. Now think about the teachers who best taught you that subject. Remember how their eyes *sparkled*, almost annoyingly, with excitement? If you're honest, you'll admit that you really appreciated their enthusiasm. In fact, that's the main reason you remember them right now. It's true for teachers, and it's true for you: passion positions excellence.

Another benefit to getting excited about what you do is the satisfaction you experience when you consistently get to do something you love. On one of our flights to a California video shoot, Coby, my twin brother, saw a guy check in a handgun at the airport desk. Later, sitting in his assigned seat on the plane, Coby watched as that same guy walked down the aisle, eventually sitting right next to him. Now we all know there are

GO BIG TIP

Passion positions excellence.

two types of plane people: talkers and people who try to avoid talkers. The understatement of the year is that Coby's a talker. Not one to waste time, Coby cut straight to the point: "So . . . saw you check in a handgun. You a good guy or a bad guy?"

He was a good guy, a Houston police officer with twenty-five years on the force. His specialty: flying the helicopters used to record high-speed car chases. Now granted, that's a sick awesome job, but regardless, this guy's passion for it was undeniable. Looking out the tiny window at the clear, blue sky, he told Coby that flying on a day like that made him want to cut his vacation early and get back on the job. The whole time he talked, he smiled. He clearly couldn't help it. He loved what he did.

That's the goal.

Let me tell you how that plays out for us. We love doing trick basketball shots. It's a way for us to take on challenges thought to be difficult or even impossible. But if you think back to the last chapter, you'll remember how that passion was born from another: competition. If there's one thing that describes hanging out at our house in College Station, Texas, it has to be this idea of constant competition. That competition is what drove us to keep taking shots for our first video, and it's what continues to drive us today. When we attempt a trick shot, we aren't just competing against each other; we're competing against every shot we've ever made. And that's what keeps us excited and pushes us to go big.

Your passions probably don't involve throwing a basketball off frighteningly tall places. For you, they might look more like cooking, building things with your hands, playing music, coaching a sport, solving difficult equations, running fast,

HUSTLE BALL

One of the best outlets for our competitive natures is a game we call "Hustle Ball." No matter how I try to explain the screaming, wrestling death-match of friendship that is Hustle Ball, showing you will make the most sense. For the first time ever, I present to you Hustle Ball: lots of hustle, only one ball.

DudePerfect.com

taking pictures, having pictures taken of you, or maybe, like me, writing about cool stuff.

Whatever it is, for most of us, it's not too difficult to come up with a few answers to the *what do you like to do* question. Yes, it's fairly easy to identify things we're passionate about. And while it's nice to simply enjoy your passions, I'd like you to consider giving purpose to one of those passions. If you haven't done it already, I think it's time to transform one of your passions into a dream, one you can pursue in a Go Big way.

Now, I could waste time trying to convince you how great it would be to choose, chase, and achieve your dream, but I'm guessing you're already convinced. In fact, that's probably why you're holding this book. So let's dive right in.

So far, you've thought about a couple of different passions in your life, but in order to lock in on that chaseable dream, the first thing you have to do is narrow your focus. It's time to put your passions on a plate and choose one.

I suggest you start by asking yourself these simple questions: *What am I most passionate about? What do I enjoy most? What is most exciting to me? What is most energizing for me?*

Only *you* can measure your smile when it comes to each one. In other words, only *you* can truly answer those questions. What you're drawn to is important, but there's one more crucial question you need to consider as you're choosing from your passions: *Is it reasonable for me to pursue this passion?*

Now before you answer that, let me make myself clear. I'm not asking if this passion is reasonable within your current situation. I'm not asking if you have the time or resources to pursue this passion. No, I'm asking if you have the natural gifts necessary to pursue it. In other words, have you had success in this area in the past? Have others confirmed your talent in this area? This is a hard question to answer—and it's not always fun. But in answering it, you will either save yourself time and heartache, or you'll find an increased level of confidence as you move forward. No doubt about it, this is a question that requires brutal honesty. But if you can answer *yes*—and not an *American Idol*, "obviously my baby girl can sing" yes, but an honest yes—then you're ready to move on.

It's early, so we don't need to talk about your business plan—yet. In chapter 5, we'll talk about finding your niche and monetizing it. Right now, we still need to narrow that passion of yours toward a specific, chaseable dream. We still need to form a mental picture of what it is you're going to go big after. And we'll continue toward that goal by asking two more questions.

First, since we already know *what* you like to do, now it's time to find out *who* you like to experience that *with*. In other words, when you picture your dream, is it a one-man show, or are others a part of it with you? Our dream was a team effort right from the beginning, but not everyone's is. We'll talk about this more in the next chapter, but no matter which direction you choose, this aspect of "team" is one that needs to be explored early and often.

The second question follows suit. You've already answered the questions *what* and *who with*. Now you need to answer this question: *Who for?* In other words, *Who do you see appreciating what it is that you do? Who is your most likely audience, community, and consumer base?* Obviously you don't need to have all the answers here, but as you can imagine, it's beneficial to envision the type of interest that may or may not surround your goods or services. The cool part is that your guesses at these questions,

TRICK SHOOTING 101

Investing in a Sheetrock repair class is a great decision if trick shooting and competition find their way into your home.

whether they're based on anything factual or not, will provide you with a more concrete picture of what your dream could be. And a dream, at this point, is exactly what you're aiming for.

It doesn't have to be perfect, but by now you should have a fairly clear picture of the dream you want to chase. And whether you just discovered this dream during the last few pages or you've been envisioning it for years, it's time to answer the most important question yet: *What now?*

The key to taking your passion to the next level, the key to launching off toward your dream, is to discover your niche. *That*, in my opinion, is the most important thing, especially for a business-minded dream. So, with a dream in mind, how do you find your niche? More in-depth answers to that question are coming in chapter 5, but in order to get started, let's discuss a couple of practical ways to move toward your niche—and ultimately, your dream.

The first suggestion I have is to intentionally engage your passion with your dream in mind. Your dream is probably cloudy; everyone's is at first. But if you will align your passion with your dream, you will naturally begin to see where you best fit. Try to notice, for example, the part of your passion that most excites you. If your passion is baking, are you most enthusiastic about following the recipe, the preparation, the decoration, or the pleased reactions of those you share the finished product with? Your answer to this question could point you more specifically toward your area of involvement within your particular passion. Why? As I said earlier, when you're excited about what you do, you're in the best possible position for excellence. The motivation here is that when you're looking for potential payment within this passion, it's essential to identify the area in which you have the most to offer. From experience, I suggest you start in the area you're most excited about. Someone will likely be willing to pay you either for your excellence at the task or for your eagerness to perform the task. Either way, your excitement for that task has put you in a desirable position.

As you engage your passion in this way, you will also see holes you could potentially fill. As I've said before, we believe that you can make money pursuing your passion. So as you practice your passion with your dream in mind, look for areas where you feel qualified to either improve or completely revo-lutionize the system currently in place. Look for areas where the system lacks in excellence, and see if you can use your natural skills to find a solution. That's where the money is—in the niche *you* can fill.

By exploring your passion—its areas of greatest interest to you, as well as its areas of apparent need—you can zero in on a dream that not only sounds fun but also has the potential for profit.

It may not feel like it yet, but shaping your dream in your mind is a huge step toward achieving it in real life. And now that we've made that crucial mental step, it's time to really get going.

GO BIG TIP

That's where the money is—in the niche *you* can fill.

BUILDING YOUR TEAM

A couple of years ago, the other Dude Perfect guys and I talked about how cool it would be to put something on YouTube that hit a million views. So when we launched our first basketball video, we knew this was probably our best chance to make that happen. At the time, I was the only one with a YouTube account, so we uploaded the video under my YouTube channel name, "corycotton." Looking back, it's weird we didn't create a new account for Dude Perfect, but hey, the fact that it all ended up being under my name is—how should I say this—*awesome*.

We put the video online because we wanted our families and friends to see it. We were proud of the way it turned out, and we thought it was something unique that people would enjoy. But like I said, we also wanted to hit our one-million-view goal. We figured the smartest thing to do was to push it hard from the very beginning. So once the video was uploaded to YouTube, we did what any college student would do: We got on Facebook and told everyone we knew about it. We posted the video link on our own Facebook walls and sent it to all our best friends. Our approach was simple: "Help our video hit a million views!" Asking others to help, inviting them into this dream with us, turned out to be the best thing we could have done.

Almost immediately our video gained serious momentum. Our Facebook friends not only watched it, but they sent it to their own friends, who passed it on to everyone they knew, and on and on it went. Because of this growing support base, the video gained tens of thousands of views in only a couple of days. It felt great. We were well on our way to reaching our goal.

In those early days, we realized something that has stayed with us. When we invited others to pursue the one-million-view goal with us, they really came through. A small part of that may be because they knew us, but really, the numbers grew way too quickly for that to be the case. The truth is that people love to leave their mark on something big. Even if their role is fairly small, people like to help shape something that stands out, something that itself is impressive. The fact that we already had a one-million-view goal in the first place is, granted, a little crazy, but it's big goals like this that inspire others to jump on board. In our situation, and in yours, we believe that with enough inspiration, anyone will want to play a part. And as we've seen time and time again, when you're trying to go big, every role matters.

One of the best parts of Dude Perfect has been getting to work with some of my closest friends. What's made it even better is that each of our strengths fills in the gaps where the others lack. Between us, we've got visionaries, realists, artists, communications specialists, financial brains, creative minds, and plenty of what we call "fun-havers." Our differences work well together, and it has been a blast to see what each guy brings to the table.

We all know that different people are good at different things. But here's the application we don't always think about: your *hate* is someone else's *hobby*. Remember the passionate teacher example from earlier? While you grew up hating that subject, your teacher grew up studying it . . . for fun. That idea still blows my mind.

In the last part of the Get Excited section, I want to explain the best way for you to protect your excitement. The guys and I have found that one of the keys to protecting the excitement necessary to fuel our efforts is for each of us to avoid, as much as possible, the tasks that we find especially draining. For example, I hate the minutiae of event planning. I think that's because I'm more of a big picture guy, but whatever the reason, I know it hurts my head. Sean, however, thrives in the world of details. Not only is he skilled in this area, but he actually *enjoys* seeing the details fall into place.

I can still remember when I was in charge of some of the detailed tasks within Dude Perfect. I did what I had to do, but I hated it. Finally, I couldn't take it anymore, so I bravely asked Sean to help me with some of my detail-oriented jobs. I was waiting for a "Yeah, right; I've got plenty on my plate" response, but instead I heard, "Okay."

I turned around and looked behind me; I thought he was talking to someone else.

Weird, I thought. *I'm the only other person here. I guess he misunderstood me.*

So I asked him again, speaking slower this time. Laughing at the look on my face, he said, "Yeah, I heard you the first time,

GO BIG TIP

Your *hate* is someone else's *hobby.*

Cory. I'll do it. I don't mind . . . seriously. Are you ready for lunch yet?"

That was one of the greatest days of my life. And Sean kept his word. As time went on, I watched him almost effortlessly smash the work I had to sweat bullets to complete. That day I told myself that never again would I drain myself doing tasks the right person would practically steal from me if he or she knew they were available. I've already said it, but I don't care: that might have been the greatest day ever.

This is a simple concept, but it's one that is overlooked far too often. Sean is not only gifted at details—in reality he is *drawn* to them. I could have done the detail work, but it would have drained my energy and left me in a horrible position to help the team. Instead, by having Sean handle our detail-oriented tasks, the work was done efficiently, and most important, it was done with excellence. And whereas tasks like these would have undoubtedly worn me out, they didn't affect Sean in the same way. Sean naturally has an interest in details, so his efforts, believe it or not, actually energized him.

So as you set off down the Go Big path, think about how certain tasks affect you. Which ones drain you? Which ones do you enjoy most? Which ones energize you? With those answers in mind, now think about what you spend the majority of your time and effort doing. You probably know where I'm going with this, but I'll say it anyway: If you're not spending most of your time doing something that energizes you, you're not only holding out on yourself—you're holding out on those around you. If this is you, you have much more to offer than what you're currently contributing, and you know it.

If you're not where you want to be, chances are you're not

SEAN

Dude Perfect started with six of us. At the end of 2010, Sean, a studly doctor-to-be, stepped down in order to better pursue med school. He's still one of our best friends, and we miss him and his detailed mind in the group. Coby— our next most detailed thinker—took over his role. We wish Sean all the best. He's the man.

super excited about that. You may or may not be responsible for the position you're in, but you have the opportunity to reevaluate right now, to set a new course, and then to do something about it. That's what this book is all about.

When we're somewhere we don't want to be, the tendency is to think of ourselves as victims of our circumstances. We can't do that. With all that we have, we must resist that train of thought. See, the *victim* mind-set and the *Go Big* mind-set are exact opposites. A victim feels sorry for himself; a Go Big person intentionally pursues a better situation. A victim wallows; a Go Big person takes action.

My guess is that you do want to take action, you do want to go big, but maybe, as you've been reading about this whole team thing—and my team in particular—you're rolling your eyes, thinking, *Five willing-to-help teammates? Must be nice.* Maybe you don't have eager, talented people lining up to help you chase your dream. Maybe, when it comes down to it, you feel all alone in your Go Big pursuit. Well, if that's you, take a deep breath. I promise that having no one else in the "office" with you doesn't mean you have to be alone.

Remember the "your hate is someone else's hobby" idea I talked about earlier? Here's where that really comes into play. Often, whether you're by yourself or not, you'll realize there's a piece or two missing from your team. Here's my suggestion: instead of trying to fill that gap yourself, look for an outside person who you know is passionate in that particular area and see if that person would volunteer some time to help you out. It sounded unrealistic to me, too, until we gave it a try.

Days after our first video was uploaded to YouTube, Coby and I were sitting on the couch watching the Masters golf

GO BIG TIP

If you're not spending most of your time doing something that energizes you, you're not only holding out on yourself— you're holding out on those around you.

tournament. Computers in our laps, we were laughing about the hilarious comments people were leaving on our video. At some point, Coby looked at me and said, "We need another place for people to talk about this video. Why don't we make our own website? I wonder if DudePerfect.com is available."

It was—for about ten more minutes, the time it took us to figure out how to buy our own domain name. Coby proudly texted the rest of the guys, "Congrats, fellas. You're one of six people in the world who own DudePerfect.com." We'd made our first-ever Internet real estate purchase, and it felt great.

Along with creating our own website—which we did through a program called iWeb on our Mac—we reserved some Gmail e-mail addresses so people could reach out to us or ask us questions. We then posted all this info in the description section of our increasingly hot YouTube video.

As the views continued to climb, people wrote in—lots of people. Most wanted to tell us how much they loved the video, which was extremely encouraging. But in addition to those types of comments, we got messages we hadn't expected—from the media. From all over the country, they wrote in to see if we'd do a radio interview with their particular station or reply to a couple of their questions. The requests came in quickly and in bulk. We were absolutely blown away. And we had no idea how to respond.

After an hour or so of staring at the computer, we realized it was really dumb to just let these important e-mails sit unanswered. We decided to ask for some serious business help. We knew that Tyler's dad was a killer businessman, a guy who'd previously worked in public relations and was currently a high-level software salesman. We'd always laughed at the way he explained his sales work to us: "I take people's money and give them stuff . . . in that order."

So, with this crazy influx of requests piling up, we asked for his help. He—like Sean earlier—gladly accepted, and in doing so, made a choice that ended up changing his life as much as ours.

A minute ago, I used the description "fun-haver." Well, we've got another one: "work-doer." This selective category is for people you can always count on, people who make things happen, people you always want playing for you, not against you. These are people like Jack Bauer, Maximus Decimus Meridius, Oprah, and Tyler's dad, Jeff Toney, also known as "Mr. T."

Trust me, you'll hear more stories about Mr. T—the man, the myth, the legend—later. He's helped and supported us more than we can ever explain. So why did he agree to help us out? Why was he so willing? Well, we believe there are a few simple reasons why he said yes. First of all, he's Tyler's dad. No one would deny that this was a helpful fact, but as I remember, being Tyler's dad hadn't persuaded him to do Tyler's physics homework. No, there was more to it than that. The second reason was that he knew we needed him. That was obvious. It might have taken him a full five seconds to see how lost we were when it came to the business side of things. He saw the gap, and with his sales and public relations background, he knew he could fill it. Finally—and most important to us and to you—there was the *excitement* factor. On one hand, he was drawn in by *our excitement*. Our excitement was more than appealing; it was contagious. On the other hand, *he* was excited about our potential from the very beginning. He was passionate about what we were asking him to do, and he was excited about the venture itself. Our excitement drew him in, and his excitement

MR. T

Could there be a cooler business manager name than Mr. T? When we're on conference calls, we try to be professional and call him Jeff, but sometimes we slip up: "On our end, we've got Coby, Tyler, Sam—our lawyer—and our business manager, Mr. T." We didn't realize it at first, but it turns out that you can hear fear over the phone.

sealed the deal. And we couldn't be happier to have him. From the beginning, he helped us recognize the significance of what was happening. He knew it was worth our time, and apparently—since he said yes—it was also worth his.

Earlier I said we've asked for help from lots of people. That was an understatement. At no point did we think we could do this alone. Some people try to do everything by themselves. That was never our approach. Over the last two years we've gotten help and advice from lawyers, CPAs, merchandise professionals, moms, dads, web developers, athletes, children, musicians, other YouTubers, pastors, friends, NBA agents, brand consultants, and many, many more. We got crucial business advice from men and women who had started their own companies, who had worked with friends, and who had made mistakes and had experiences that they desperately wanted us to avoid. If your team isn't strong in a crucial area, please ask around. Yes, we've paid some of these people at certain times, but for a while, they simply volunteered.

Take our website, for example. While we watched the Masters, Coby and I made the best website we knew how, but the final product was pretty sad. About a week later, however, we got an exciting e-mail. It was from an independent web developer, a guy who'd seen our video and landed on our poor excuse for a website. He said our content was so engaging that he'd be willing to create a better site for us for free. He explained that the traffic and exposure our website could give his company was incentive enough for him to help us out. We looked at some of the other work he had done, and it was clear the guy was good. It was a great offer, and we needed the help, so we gratefully accepted. Within a matter of weeks, DudePerfect.com had a much-improved new look.

In both of these cases—Mr. T and the web developer—our excitement drew them in, and their excitement sealed the deal. And that has consistently been our experience. As you're building your team, focus on the excitement factor, both yours and that of the person you're asking for help. Remember that your excitement will naturally attract people to assist you in pursuing your passion. And remember that their excitement will show up positively in their work.

Here's this chapter's simple but life-changing take-away: Ask people for help. If you've got an exciting dream, others are going to want to jump into that process with you. If you need help in a certain area, ask someone you know who is qualified to help out there. People love to have their gifts and skills affirmed, and there's no better way to do that than to invite them to help you fill a certain gap. It's great for you, and it's great for them. It's a win-win. The key is to actually ask. In our case, Mr. T had some motivation to help us out, but at the end of the day, he didn't help us just because we needed it; he helped us because we asked him. So take your dream and all the excitement that surrounds it and build your team. The only reason they're not already lined up is because they're waiting to be invited.

GOOD MORNING AMERICA

Four days after our first video launched, a producer from Good Morning America *asked if we would appear on the show. We called Mr. T, and he explained how to handle the interview. Then he said, "Guys, I think you've really got something here."*

I remember thinking, If Mr. T believes in us, this must be worth pursuing. He was right.

PART TWO

OWN IT

CHAPTER 4
MEETING LEBRON

When you're truly excited about what you're doing—or what you'll soon be doing—then you're ready for our next Go Big principle: Own It. If you ask me, this is where your journey really gets fun. Over the next few chapters, we're going to dive into all that this principle means for you, but for now, just think about it like this: to own it means to fully embrace and relentlessly pursue your vision.

We'll get into what "fully embracing and relentlessly pursuing your vision" means in more detail in this and the coming chapters. Right now, think about it this way: when you truly own your Go Big dream, you'll want to share it with others.

What follows is an example—granted, an extreme one—of what it means to fully embrace your vision. It's the story of how I, in person, showed Dude Perfect to LeBron James.

Where we last left off, our first video was blowing up online. Not wanting to be a one-hit wonder, we raised the bar with a sequel video filmed at Tyler's family's ranch, and as we went our

DudePerfect.com

separate ways for the summer, Dude Perfect: Ranch Edition was cruising toward its one millionth hit.

I was in San Diego, California, with an organization called Campus Crusade for Christ. I spent most of my time there on the University of California at San Diego (UCSD) campus, hanging out with students and hosting Bible studies. One day, a couple of my friends and I saw a sign advertising the LeBron James King's Academy basketball camp. Incredibly pumped, we knew we had to see him. As we walked toward the rec center—the hardwood throne room—we pictured ourselves living the dream in what would surely be our first-name-basis future with LeBron.

Reality set in, however, when we got to the gym. We weren't registered and weren't high school students or even students of UCSD, so getting in was going to be harder than we'd thought. I was devastated for about a second, but as it turns out, I'm a big fan of LeBron, less a fan of failure, and King James was still on the other side of the wall.

After a few false starts, I took the direct approach: I asked for a visitor's pass to look around the rec center. Being a loyal student of Texas A&M University, I wasn't really in the market for a transfer, but hey, it never hurts to keep your options open.

As we passed through the turnstile and into the rec center, I noticed this weird feeling, like something was pulling me along. It was greatness, and it was coming from the gym.

We walked up to some large windows. To our surprise, there wasn't a single high school student in the gym. Instead, with the day's camp hours completed, LeBron James, Mo Williams, and a few other players and coaches from the Cleveland Cavaliers were having a private practice session.

We'd made it. We could see LeBron . . . kind of. Unfortunately, there were window blinds covering certain sections of our view, so no matter how hard we tried, we could only see slices of the action. King James drove the lane, took off toward the rim, and with authority, probably dunked. Probably . . . because an unappreciative window blind was sitting in my front-row seat.

We were disappointed with the view, but content nonetheless. We'd set out to see LeBron, and we did. About five minutes later, a bodyguard looked our direction from inside the gym. We were sure he was going to tell us to leave—to find some other NBA legend to watch—but he didn't. He said LeBron wanted to know if we'd like to come in.

Would the six of us like to be the only audience in the gym with LeBron? Um, yes.

Trying to keep our smiles inside our mouths, we followed the bodyguard inside and sat down on the sideline. Now only a few feet from the action, the tables had turned; the blinds were jealous. For at least thirty minutes, the players shot, dunked, and drilled more intensely than any practice I'd ever seen or been a part of. It was a ridiculously impressive showcase of talent.

Over the course of the practice, the bodyguard had let in a few other "witnesses," as Nike calls them, and as the practice came to a close, those viewers filtered out. I watched person after person head straight for the door, each passing up the opportunity to shake hands with James, or to at least try. As for me, I was completely unfazed by the choking crowd. In my mind, there were only two people in that gym: LeBron and me.

As soon as we'd entered the gym, I'd hoped I'd get to meet him. If that had been my only goal, I'll admit I might have joined the crowd and walked away. But it wasn't my only goal.

DRILLS WITH THE KING

My favorite drill was a four-player shooting exercise. From three to four feet behind the college arc—simulating a deep NBA three-pointer—the players shot, rounding the perimeter. If two of them missed from a spot, they would have to start over. But the drill lasted at least ten minutes . . . and they never started over. When the pressure was on, they fired shot after shot—swish every time.

Standing there on the sideline, a thought hit me: I had our Dude Perfect: Ranch Edition video cued up on my iPhone. The ridiculous idea was only halfway in my mind, but already I was smiling. I wanted to laugh, but I had to keep myself together. This was a huge moment. I had just realized that I could personally show Dude Perfect to LeBron James. If he didn't know about Dude Perfect, this was my chance to change that. Meeting him would be great. Sharing our vision with him would be a million times cooler.

It felt crazy, but the moment this idea occurred to me, I refused to settle for anything else. Fortunately, my plan was awesome. It was almost disappointing how easy this was going to be:

1. Walk up to LeBron.
2. Show him our new video . . . on my phone.
3. Become best friends.

This might be hard to believe, but there was, in fact, a flaw in my plan. When we were allowed into the gym, the bodyguard had made it clear that we were not to pull out our cameras or phones. Traditionally, I'm not much of a rule breaker, but blinded by my desire to show Dude Perfect to King James, I decided to risk it. My feet started walking before my mind weighed the consequences. I was halfway across the court when it occurred to me that I might get shot. But if my mind hesitated, my legs didn't. Focused on the goal, I powered past the thought of getting shot, replacing it with a much cooler one: *If LeBron can have "no regard for human life," I can too.*

I was about ten feet away now. LeBron was still stretching,

lying on his stomach, with a trainer helping him stretch his legs. My timing, at this point, became crucial. See, as I'd begun walking, so had that bodyguard. I saw him out of the corner of my eye, and as I made my final few steps toward LeBron, I put myself on the hit list: I reached for my phone.

That probably wasn't the smartest thing to do, but I did it, and I have to be completely honest with you: it was smooth. In one fluid motion, like I'd trained for that moment my whole life, I knelt down to LeBron's face level, slid my phone from my pocket, started the video, and said, "Hey, LeBron. My name's Cory. I go to school at Texas A&M, and my roommates and I made a trick shot basketball video that's gone big on YouTube. I thought you'd like to check it out."

My heart was pounding, but everything seemed okay. I'd reached LeBron only moments ahead of the bodyguard, just long enough for me to say what I had and tilt the video in his direction. Confused but clearly intrigued, he glanced down at the screen in time to see Tyler's hook shot from the top of the ranch's feed tower. LeBron cracked up laughing. He grabbed the phone from my hand so he could see it closer. As you can imagine, I was loving this. But—it didn't last. The bodyguard stepped between us and forcefully told me I had to leave.

I don't remember being mad; I knew he was just doing his job. But I don't remember being appreciative, either. Actually, I have no idea what I felt, because there wasn't enough time. As I looked at the man responsible for crushing my hopes and dreams, I heard another voice, one frighteningly similar to LeBron James's. Standing back up, I turned just in time to witness LeBron's mouth move as he raised his head away from my phone's screen. "Nah, man, he's cool."

NO REGARD FOR HUMAN LIFE

youtube.com/watch?v=9MSQ_G5MZFo

Shocked but trying to keep a straight face, I glanced over at my friends. I knew we were all thinking the same thing: *That just happened.* With the bodyguard fresh off the case and LeBron's focus back on the video, others decided their jobs could wait as well. The trainer paused LeBron's stretches to get a better view of the phone. Two of LeBron's friends, the guys from the State Farm dancing commercial, who I just noticed were there, also crowded around. LeBron and his crew had stopped everything to smile, laugh, comment on, and enjoy Dude Perfect: Ranch Edition.

We talked and laughed about Dude Perfect for a while, LeBron saying stuff like, "That's real cool, man, real cool." Knowing he had to get back to his stretches, I looked him in the eye, let his hand swallow mine in a handshake, and said, "All right, LeBron, take care, man. God bless."

Now that experience may not have radically changed me as a person, but as far as Dude Perfect goes, it was a defining moment for me. When the fog cleared, I realized that in spite of my nerves, I'd shown one of our Dude Perfect videos to LeBron James, the guy who reinvented basketball. See, none of the other guys were there that day; I was the only one. But through my actions, I proved to LeBron, the other Dude Perfect guys, and more importantly to myself that I really believe in what we're doing. I'd embraced our vision, and it had created in me the willingness to take action.

And I didn't know it yet, but I wasn't the only Dude Perfect member owning our vision that summer.

While I was meeting LeBron, Cody and Tyler were in Texas working at a Christian summer camp called Sky Ranch. And since the camp had so many cool things for the kids to do, Ty and Cody made time to film summer camp–style trick shots from

LEBRON'S DNA

Outside the gym, I noticed something glimmering on my phone: a fingerprint, way bigger than mine. I can't explain my next thought, but anyone who loves basketball will understand. LeBron James is arguably the greatest player ever. His fingerprint was on my phone. So . . . I licked it. Am I bigger, stronger, and faster than before? Yes. I have MVP DNA in my bloodstream. Deal with it.

every camp object you can imagine: a zipline, a blob, a golf cart, a trapeze, a trampoline, and many more. It was an incredible idea; the fun camp atmosphere worked perfectly for our third major video. If you've never seen Dude Perfect: Summer Camp Edition, you're going to want to check that out—like, right now.

When I was with LeBron, I took an opportunity to share our vision with him. I owned it. When Cody and Tyler worked at summer camp, they raised the Dude Perfect bar by filming the best video yet. And with their hard work, they expanded our brand presence, both online and with the countless people they interacted with that summer. They owned it as well. And as we talked about all this, we were motivated by the understanding that, whether we were together or not, each member of the team was doing his part to pursue the greater vision.

From experiences like these, we know that one of the greatest moments in your Go Big journey will be the realization that you fully embrace what you're doing. So whatever vision you're chasing, if it's something you're truly excited about, you'll be amazed at how quickly your actions will back up your passions. Time might get away from you as you find yourself working late into the evening. Your thoughts might shift more and more to your vision's ever-increasing potential. You might even spend your money differently, considering how to best leverage it for your dream. Regardless of what it looks like for you, the important thing is that as you fully embrace your vision, your actions will follow suit.

Part of this includes sharing your vision. When people get excited about something and truly embrace it, they tell others about it. Sometimes this is easy to do—like talking about the newest and greatest movie or the hottest brand of running shoes.

DUDE PERFECT: SUMMER CAMP EDITION

DudePerfect.com

TRICK SHOOTING 101

If shooting from a summer-camp blob, there is a 50-pound weight differential rule for a reason—a 390-pound difference feels as big as it looks.

Other times this is difficult. We like to tell others about what excites us, but sometimes we fear that others might reject what is so important to us. When rejection doesn't cost us much, we're more likely to share our excitement with others. But when we feel like the stakes are higher—because the rejected thing is a part of us—we can be less open about our excitement. Just like my experience with LeBron, it takes courage to share your vision with someone else. But also just like my experience with LeBron, if you'll do it, you just might have a great story to tell.

Start by sharing your dream with your family and close friends. It might feel weird to talk about it at first, but we think you'll be surprised by the positive reactions you'll receive. If you're having a hard time bringing it up, we've found that the easiest way to talk about your own dream is to first ask others about theirs. Everyone has a dream, and most people love to talk about themselves. In other words, this is easier than talking about the weather. Try it.

Once you've done that, begin to share your vision in everyday situations. If you travel often, strike up conversations with the people beside you on the bus or plane. If you don't travel, use your lunch break as a good time to ask colleagues about their dreams. Use those open doors to discuss your Go Big dream. You'll be amazed at others' dreams, as well as the positive affirmation you'll receive.

When I showed our video to LeBron, it proved that I was already excited about what we were doing. But his genuine enjoyment of it—*that* fed my fire like nothing before. No doubt about it, when I stepped out of that gym and into the California sunlight, I was more excited about Dude Perfect than I'd ever been.

CHAPTER 5

CASHING IN

This chapter is about making money. It's about leveraging your Go Big dream for an income stream. It's possible that you're not interested in that, and that's fine. What I'm sure you're interested in is achieving your dream—and I know that because you're still reading this book. I also know that your unique vision is, obviously, different from the rest of ours. You might want to start a business, for example, while another reader might have her sights set on qualifying for the next Olympics. Either way, you both want to go big, and we respect that a hundred percent.

Whether your dream includes a monetary component or not, this chapter is well worth the read. I'm the first to admit that this book is more about achieving your dream than making money. But I also believe that in this connected world there *is* a potential for income within your unique dream. Some dreams hide this potential better than others, but I think everyone can make money somewhere within their dream. The key is to identify your niche.

If you remember, we defined the Own It principle like this: fully *embrace* and relentlessly *pursue* your vision. We've touched on the embrace aspect, and in this and the next chapter, I want to spend some time on the idea of relentless pursuit.

I won't deny it. Let it be said; let it be written: I love the word *relentless*. Maybe it's because I'm a testosterone-filled guy, but something inside me stirs when I think about someone relentlessly doing anything. Think about it. Who are the best fighters? The relentless ones. Which defensive backs do quarterbacks hate the most? The relentless ones. Now flip it—which quarterback does every defensive back hate the most? Brett Favre, of course, the most relentless one. The best basketball teams, superheroes, global leaders, private investigators, and competitors in the World's Strongest Man competition are all, without exception, relentless.

And *that* is exactly how Go Big dreams—the most epic dreams out there—have to be pursued. Although that sounds great, by now you probably have two questions:

1. What does *relentless pursuit* actually look like?
2. What happened to the money you mentioned earlier?

We've found that there's one main answer to both of these questions: *find your niche.* Once you do that, you'll be able to focus your efforts and potentially see a profit, as well.

As we launched into our Go Big journey, our niche was clear. The night we uploaded our first video, we searched for trick basketball shots on YouTube. We could count the results on

GO BIG TIP

Whether you want to make money doing something you love or you're simply pursuing your dream, finding your niche is the key.

one hand, and in our opinion, the few videos that did surface weren't very engaging. We wanted to make a crazy basketball shot video, but unlike the others, we wanted it to be exciting to watch. More than anything, we wanted each viewer's experience to reflect the fun we had while making the shots. That's why we put music in the background and left in the ridiculous celebrations after we made each basket. We wanted to draw the viewer into all the competitive excitement we'd discovered that sunny afternoon in our backyard. On the computer screen that night, we saw a gaping hole in YouTube. As we huddled around the search results page, we found our niche.

Whether you want to make money doing something you love or you're simply pursuing your dream, finding your niche is the key. Without a niche, no matter how relentless your pursuit, you'll chase too many rabbit trails, run out of energy, and make little progress—and even less money. But finding your niche will bring the moneymaking opportunities to you.

After the successful release of our second video, Dude Perfect: Ranch Edition, we received an interesting e-mail from the producers of a television show called *Country Fried Home Videos*, a show that airs on CMT (Country Music Television) channel. The e-mail asked us one simple question: would we be willing to license our Ranch Edition video for use in one of their upcoming episodes? We had no idea what to think about this request, so we forwarded it to Mr. T and asked for his "is this a scam?" expertise.

Although the e-mail in question was much more professional-sounding than a typical scam e-mail, we were still skeptical that a television show would offer to pay us so they could play our

SCAM E-MAILS

We get lots of scam e-mails. You know what we're talking about:

Congratulations! You just won a gazillion dollars in the Brazilian-Chinese-Pan-American Lottery! Claim your winnings by giving us all your personal information so we can quickly trade our fake money for your real money.

If we had a dollar for every lottery we "won," we could host our own.

video during one of their episodes. But if it was legit, that'd be the coolest thing ever.

Until this point, the only money we'd made was from Google AdSense—those advertisements that pop up on some of the YouTube videos you watch. And how much money were we talking about here? Well, let's just say that we had considered framing our first six pennies. We weren't putting ourselves through school, or even a Wendy's drive-thru. (Of course, that would change in the future, but at the beginning, we were definitely open to other ways of making a little extra cash.)

Then we got a call from Mr. T. He was fresh off the phone with some of the TV show's producers. Happy birthday, Dude Perfect. It was legit.

We were floored. We couldn't believe someone wanted to pay us for our video. It felt too good to be true. Someone was offering to pay us for something we'd made just for fun.

But as more of these offers came in, we began to realize that people wanted to use our content for a reason: it was unique. When we made our first basketball video, we were doing something we loved. But in the process, we identified a unique gap—a niche—in the YouTube world, and we filled it.

And the most exciting part was that our niche was much larger than we had first thought. The same gap we'd seen on YouTube was also present in the traditional media. The overarching niche was in the creation of the crazy basketball shot content itself. With the videos in circulation online, we soon found out that television, radio, newspaper, and magazine outlets were interested as well.

The moral here is simple: *find your niche, and your clients will find you.*

GO BIG TIP

Find your niche, and your clients will find you.

I realize we're not the first people to emphasize the importance of finding your niche. The difference here is that from what we've seen and experienced, we know your niche is best found in the natural outpourings of who you are, of your instinctive passions and strengths. Since you are unique, we believe you have something unique to offer. If you have a dream, you have a niche.

That sounds good, I know, but if you're still struggling with finding your niche, if you still haven't discovered what it is you have to offer, I want to help you.

Below is a list of questions that will not only help you move toward identifying your unique niche but will help you identify potential customers as well. We've asked ourselves many of these practical questions throughout our process. They've helped us, and I think they'll help you, too.

Take a few minutes to write down your answers to these questions. I promise it will be worth your time. Last thing: since this is essentially a brainstorming procedure, think big. In the world of creativity, no idea is ever too big. Ever.

Why do you do what you do?

_____

_____

_____

_____

_____

_____

GO BIG TIP

If you have a dream, you have a niche.

What part of your dream is novel or refreshing to the culture around you?

_____

_____

_____

_____

_____

What do you have to offer that you've rarely or never seen offered before?

_____

_____

_____

_____

_____

What do you bring to market that is better than what is already there?

_____

_____

_____

_____

_____

_____

What part of your dream is forward-thinking?
Are you reacting or preacting?

_____

_____

_____

_____

_____

_____

How will others benefit from what you have to offer?

_____

_____

_____

_____

_____

_____

Who is your target audience? Who do you want it to be?

_____

_____

_____

_____

_____

GO BIG TIP

If making money for yourself is the ultimate goal for your vision, you need a much bigger vision.

What can you combine with your dream to form a niche worth paying for? What outlets are ideal for what you offer? (For example, we took our passion—crazy basketball shots— and combined it with a distribution method, YouTube, and that ended up forming a niche.)

_____

_____

_____

_____

_____

What population can your services bring to other services? In other words, what is the advertising potential of your dream?

_____

_____

_____

_____

_____

_____

As you combine your unique passions and strengths, I believe you will find your niche, one that people will be willing to pay for. And with your niche in sight, you'll have the focus necessary to relentlessly pursue your vision. You'll truly be able to own it.

Here's the deal. We know you have a dream. We also know it's possible for you to find your niche. Finally, we know that if you do find your niche, there's a good chance people will be willing to pay for it. But while getting paid to do something we love has been awesome, the money has never been our focus, and it shouldn't be yours, either. If making money for yourself is the ultimate goal for your vision, you need a much bigger vision.

So keep your overall focus on the dream. And don't worry. If you're achieving excellence within your niche, opportunities for income will arise. When they do, take them. Finding an income stream within your dream can support the efforts that instinctively excite you. It's a wonderful cycle. Making money allows you to continue doing what you love to do.

CHAPTER 6

WORLD RECORDS ARE COOL

After our summer apart, we were excited to be back at school. Maybe not about the homework part, but definitely about the being there part. In some ways, it felt just like it used to. We signed up for classes, dusted off our bikes, got parking passes, and got our schedules figured out. On top of that, the campus hadn't changed much, our next-door neighbors still lived there, and as always, it was Texas-hot outside. Everything around us seemed exactly the same, but we felt different.

We acted like we didn't know the reason, but of course we did. It was hard to explain to the people around us, but in a very real way, our lives *were* different. Every single day, on top of school stuff, we were planning and managing all our Dude Perfect stuff.

A few weeks into the school year, Coby and Tyler were driving home after a day on campus. On their way they passed Kyle Field, Texas A&M's huge football stadium. As Tyler looked at it through his window, he said to Coby, "I really think I could shoot from the top of the stands down to the football field."

"Ty, that might be the dumbest thing you've ever said."

When they got home, Tyler told all of us his idea, and we all laughed. But we realized Tyler wasn't joking. He was dead serious, and our doubts were making him want the shot even more.

After Ty did some more persuading, Coby sent an e-mail to a few people in the A&M athletic department, asking if it would be possible for us to shoot a basketball from the top of their famous stadium. A couple of days later, we got a surprising e-mail from the athletic department. First off, they agreed with most of us, saying there was no way it was possible. But they also said something else. They said yes. We *could* use Kyle Field to try the impossible feat. Extremely excited, we arranged a good time to use the stadium.

The day we went was supposed to be just an experiment. See, the other part to this story is that a week or two earlier, ESPN had contacted us to film an *E:60* segment about the other videos we'd done. So after we got permission to use the stadium, we realized ESPN might be able to film the big moment. With approval from the athletic department, we went to the stadium to make sure the shot was doable before we told ESPN the trip would be worth their time.

Rolling up to open gates, we unloaded the goal and wheeled it in. If you've ever seen the movie *Hoosiers*, there's a classic moment when the small-town boys' basketball team arrives at the state tournament. Stepping foot inside the largest arena they've ever seen, they are overwhelmed by the enormity of the situation. As the echoing gymnasium leaves them speechless, all they can do is stare up at the stands that will soon be filled

TRICK SHOOTING 101

Never take "practice shots." In the trick shot world, if the camera's not rolling, you shouldn't be shooting.

with people watching their every move. For us, walking inside Kyle Field had that same feeling of awe. We looked around at the immensity of the place. From the ground it looked even bigger than from our usual place high up in the stands. It was epic. We couldn't help but laugh at the awesome ridiculousness of the moment. There we were, goal in tow, setting up a shot at the stadium we'd been cheering in for years.

Using the track, we rounded the perfectly green field, arrived at the fifty-yard line, and faced the goal toward the student section. The idea was pretty simple: from as high in the stands as possible, throw the ball down to the goal by the field. Kyle Field has three decks, and we thought the second deck was going to be the perfect place to shoot from. Tired of planning, we sent Tyler and Coby up the circular ramp to the second deck of the student section above. Tyler took the four basketballs we'd purchased since our first video, and Coby took a camera. Even though this was practice, we weren't going to miss the moment if something crazy happened.

Standing by the rail of the second level of the stadium, close to fifty yards away from the goal, Tyler faced the camera and said, "This is the Kyle Field shot." With his quarterback cannon, Ty unleashed the first shot . . . and three seconds later, it sailed clear over the backboard. We yelled up at him, "Are you kidding me!" To make sure he'd really just thrown it that far, Ty tried a few more times, each shot going past the goal. Through yelling up and down at each other, we all decided Tyler should move up to the incredibly high, incredibly faraway third deck of the stadium. While Tyler and Coby walked up the ramp to what would surely be too far a distance, Cody and I worked with a few of our other friends to grab the basketballs Ty had

(RE)BOUND FOR GLORY

There were some other guys there, and we welcomed their help. We chose a few rebounders and sent the rest into the stands. If Ty missed, we'd throw the ball to a guy on the first deck, who would throw it to a guy on the second deck, who would finally throw it to Coby or Ty on the third.

just launched. Needless to say, we were all still laughing about the crazy fact that we were doing this in the first place.

When they got to the top, Ty rocketed the ball from the ledge, and we all waited as the ball traveled out and down and finally landed beside the goal. We went nuts. After the more-than-four-second hang time was over, we realized that hitting a shot from that distance was actually possible. After calming down a bit, we got organized. We wanted to nail the shot, and we wanted to do it that day.

Though Tyler was getting shots near the hoop, it was harder than it looked because the ball kept curving in unexpected ways. An insane amount of wind was causing more intense curving than we'd ever experienced. And it wasn't just the speed of the wind either. Because of the stadium's bowl shape, the wind gusts were blowing one way up near the third deck and another way down by the field. The result: the ball snaked through the air and was almost impossible to aim. Almost.

DANGEROUS SHOTS

While Cody filmed below, I took on another important responsibility: protecting him from the ball. Tyler's throws blasted down, and I saw one hauling toward us. My memory is blurry, but I'm told I bailed. We laugh about it now, but Cody wasn't pleased. I apologized and didn't bail again. I wasn't going to let a trick shot kill Cody.

About thirty minutes later, Tyler was about as focused as he could be. After hitting the goal a couple of times, motivated and with adrenaline pumping, he grabbed another ball. Facing the camera, he said what we had decided was the coolest intro: "Welcome to Aggieland. This is the world's longest basketball shot." Although we hadn't yet measured the exact distance from the stands to the field, we had looked up the current record, or lack of record, and this shot would be it for sure.

Tyler took a deep breath and unleashed a missile toward the target below. The ball seemed to stay in the air forever, but as it approached, we liked its chances. We were all yelling various suggestions—in case it was listening—and the ball came crashing down, hit high on the backboard, and exploded through the net below.

Everyone went crazy. Up top, Tyler's emphatic "Yes!" mixed with Coby's disbelieving "What!" Down on the field, a few of our other friends and some of the A&M men's basketball players were there to celebrate with us. None of us could believe our eyes.

We still haven't measured the exact distance from the spot where the shot was launched to the goal below, but it's close to seventy yards. From that distance, with the type of wind we were experiencing, we thought it might never go in. But after thirty minutes of perseverance, filming, and rebounding, Tyler had nailed the shot. If you've never seen it, you need to check out both angles of our world's longest basketball shot.

In the eight months leading up to that crazy afternoon, we'd filmed Home Edition, Ranch Edition, and Summer Camp Edition, and we felt like we'd raised the bar each time. We were proud of what we'd done. We could have stayed in that pattern. Our viewers had begun to expect a certain thing from us, and it would have been easy to consistently give them that. But we didn't want to get stuck in that rut, or any rut. We were ready to raise the bar *more* than one notch at a time. We wanted to blow our old videos out of the water. We wanted to go big.

The title of this book is *Go Big: Make Your Shot Count in the Connected World*, but so far, we haven't spent much time on the *connected world* part. Here's why: Up until this point in our story, the vast influence of the connected world hadn't occurred to us—not fully, anyway.

From day one we were perfectly aware that YouTube, Facebook, Twitter, etc., were all vital to our success. And having

DUDE PERFECT: WORLD'S LONGEST BASKETBALL SHOT—3RD DECK VIEW

DudePerfect.com

DudePerfect.com

leveraged those tools, we felt, at least to a small degree, socially connected to the world. That said, it took everything that had happened so far for us to really envision the enormous potential the connected world made available to us—and not just the social networking sites, but the much larger, big-picture implications of what the connected world really meant *to us*.

With this in mind, the Kyle Field shot was really a two-part experiment for us.

First, we wanted to know if a shot like that was even possible. Truth is, we were dying to know the answer, and we were too competitive to wait for someone else to try it first.

Second, and more important, we had a theory about our YouTube videos. Our first videos were unique, but they had something else going for them as well: they stirred up familiar memories. People had made crazy front-yard basketball shots all over the world, but no one had put those types of shots together—not in a compelling way, at least. And on top of that positive familiarity, our videos were also able to offer viewers a certain "I've never seen anything like this" satisfaction.

The Kyle Field shot was a continuation of that idea. It was true that no one had ever made a shot like this on camera. That was good, and the idea of being "the first" was fairly enticing. But what we hoped would take the idea over the top was that no one had ever even *tried* a shot like that. Not on camera, not off camera. Not ever. The idea was a hundred percent fresh. It was an "I've never even considered that" idea. So although we weren't thinking in terms of the "connected world," we were curious to see what would happen if we unleashed this type of shot—this fresh, compelling content—into the online world.

The way I see it, if you're going to own it, if you're going to fully embrace and relentlessly pursue your vision, you're going to have to be willing to step out into the fresh unknown, to write part of the manual, instead of simply following one all the time.

See, a Go Big mind-set is not limited by what others have done before you. It's not limited by what others say can and can't be done. One of the main things we learned that day at Kyle Field was this: no matter the doubts, always allow uncharted territory to be more, not less, motivating. In our case, we tried to keep our focus on accomplishing what no one else had ever even attempted. So whatever your dream, remember that there is always exciting, untapped potential locked inside the unknown. Keep your focus there, not on tiny reasons for doubt.

A Go Big mind-set is not limited by perspective, either. We all know that perspective is a deceptive thing. It's like that old optical illusion: one minute you're staring at a picture of an ugly witch, but as soon as your friend points out the beautiful young woman, she's the only thing you can see. That's because perspective is relative. Therefore, be careful not to make your dream-centered decisions based solely on your own current, limited viewpoint. Make sure to consider your newfound Go Big mind-set. Often finding a better perspective is as simple as broadening your focus.

When Tyler looked at A&M's football stadium, his perspective was broader than the rest of ours. We instantly wrote off the possibility of his hitting a shot from up there, but Ty, while unsure of the potential for success, knew there was only one way to find out. In that moment, his broader perspective dramatically expanded Dude Perfect's future.

Standing inside that enormous, windy stadium, we were

GO BIG TIP

Following someone else's manual is safe, but writing your own changes the world.

confident that making the shot would set the Internet on Dude Perfect fire. The views on our other videos had proved that the basketball shot idea was compelling. But taking our YouTube identity all the way up to the top of one of the biggest football stadiums in the country—that was fancy, effective, pick-me-up-and-take-me-to-the-counter packaging. And as you'll see soon, it worked.

So wherever you are in your Go Big pursuits, you can choose to slowly improve, to slowly raise expectations, or you can choose to be different, to blow everyone's mind and grab hold of the connected-world rocket in the process. The important thing isn't just to be *different*; it's to package the content you already know is compelling in a way that will turn heads long enough for others to take notice.

The packaging part is tough. It takes focus and creativity to come up with great ideas. But it's worth every second spent. Since packaging is so important, we want to leave you with a suggestion that's a lot more useful than it sounds: to get your content noticed in the connected world, package it in a Go Big wrapper.

You and I both know that the world is drawn to a Go Big mind-set. The intangible appeal that packages success stories like Bear Grylls—the guy who takes outdoor adventure to a level most of us can only handle in an armchair—is a Go Big mind-set, a Go Big approach to life. Since you're using the principles of this Go Big process to discover your compelling vision in the first place, make sure you package that vision in a way that reflects the bigness of the idea itself.

You know your vision is great. Now the key is to get it to the masses.

GO BIG TIP

To get your content noticed in the connected world, package it in a Go Big wrapper.

Do this: look at your Go Big idea. Now apply the Go Big mind-set to it, and scale it up ten notches. By doing this, you'll be applying the Go Big mind-set to the packaging of that newest idea.

For us, our Go Big wrapper looked like this: we took our original Go Big idea of shooting and filming crazy basketball shots and decided—in order to really grab the attention of the world—to dial it up ten notches. That's where the Kyle Field shot came into play. But instead of simply calling it "The Kyle Field Shot" or "The Stadium Shot," we named it "The World's Longest Basketball Shot." Yes, we could have titled it anything we wanted, and at the end of the day, the moment would have looked the same on-screen. But the appeal to the viewer, and part of the viral attraction, was the Go Big nature of the shot's title. In other words, the packaging really helped the video catch on. Same shot, big title, more appeal.

So how would this look with you? What we'd suggest is that you take a look at your Go Big idea—the most compelling thing you have to offer—and apply to it the same thought process that we used with our world's longest shot. First, dial your compelling idea up ten notches. If you sell cupcakes, think about a way that you can really blow a certain cupcake project out of the water. To give yourself a much better chance of standing out in the crowd, do something out of the box. For example, make a hysterically large cupcake and deliver it to someone in the public spotlight. An action like that essentially packages your already compelling idea in a way that is much more likely to get noticed by the often-bored world around us. And finally, make sure you distribute that project *into* the connected world. For example, take pictures and video of the process and unleash them online. Title your video, blog, newspaper article, song, or whatever your idea is in a way that conveys the bigness of the project. The goal is simple. By stirring a flavor of bigness into your idea, you'll give it a better chance of standing out in the crowd.

CHAPTER 7

REAL APPEAL

On the Internet, maybe more than anywhere else in the world, people love to argue. On YouTube, this shows up in the comments section below a video. When our first video went live, comments flowed in like crazy. Every once in a while, we'd get a simple one-liner like, "That was incredible," or, "Wow, college students have way too much free time," but almost every single comment, hundreds in a row, debated one point: real or fake?

We've addressed this question in literally every interview we've given and probably 95 percent of the conversations we've had with people about Dude Perfect, but people keep on asking. If it's written in a published book, maybe we'll get some new questions. It's official: the shots are real.

Don't get me wrong; we're glad people think they're fake. No one would take the time to fake something that could be easily done in real life, so we take it as a compliment when people think our stuff is fake. That said, we can't help but laugh when, despite our assurances, people refuse to believe the shots actually go in.

FOR THE RECORD . . .

I want to address two frequent comments we receive:

This is obviously fake. These guys are way too good with computers. *False. If we were good enough to fake our shots, we'd be working at Pixar. It pays better.*

An electromagnetic field around the basket causes the ball to go in. *No comment. And that's not because they've figured us out.*

From day one, we decided that all of our shots would be a hundred percent real. Remember way back in chapter 1, when I was explaining how this all began for us—how we filmed our first video in the backyard? I told you about the backwards, over-the-head shot that Tyler made from one side of the yard to the other—the one that looked super fake on camera. What many people don't know is that a couple of tries before the swish you see on the video, Ty had what is often disrespect-fully called an "Aggie swish"—where the ball comes up barely short, hitting the front of the net but not actually going in. The interesting thing was that on camera, this attempt looked per-fect—it looked like it *did* go in. This was one of the first shots we'd ever done, so it was tempting to use that take and move on to the next shot. But we chose then and there to never do that. We wanted to be able to look someone in the eye and say, "Yep, they're all real, every single one." We knew that if we ever compromised, even once, we'd lose all credibility. But because we've stuck to this commitment, we can smile as hosts and radio personalities call our shots fake on the air.

We've seen firsthand just how much the world is enamored of this idea of real versus fake. Although it weirded us out at first, we think the obsession makes a lot of sense. We live in an increasingly fake world, where things are more and more often styled, staged, and scripted. So whenever something amazing happens, people assume it has to be fake. And while that is a sad reality, it's also a huge opportunity. Anyone who's pursuing a Go Big dream will have chances to take shortcuts, to fake certain elements of the work in order to arrive more quickly at the fin-ish line. But just like we've seen with our shots, authenticity is a category that can set you apart from the pack in a dramatic way.

Authenticity and a refusal to compromise lead us right into the last and final piece of the Own It principle. It's a topic that, truthfully, is difficult to talk about. But we've chosen to deal with it head-on. This chapter is about integrity.

Integrity probably wasn't the word you were expecting. That's because I described a word that was supposed to be uncomfortable to hear, yet most people don't think of integrity as off-putting or offensive. But the truth is that integrity rubs all of us the wrong way. Don't misunderstand me: we all love the *idea* of integrity. But what's dangerous is the way we treat it. Most of us, including myself, put integrity in the same category as, say, patriotism.

When I think about the word *patriotic* or see an enormous red, white, and blue flag waving in the wind, I stand a little taller, hold my head a little higher, and think to myself, *I love the US of A.* That's the fun part, and I would guess that lots of Americans react the same way. But I'd also guess that close to zero people each year belt out "God Bless America" while they file their taxes. Thinking about patriotism is great; paying the price isn't as much fun.

Integrity plays out the same way. We absolutely love it—as an idea. With roommates, coworkers, bosses, and even the occasional lawyer, we genuinely appreciate it when other people have integrity. But in our day-to-day lives, it's much more difficult to live the way we should.

You and me, we're both pursuing a Go Big dream. And if we care at all about protecting that, we have no choice but to spend real time focusing on this aspect of our character. We've seen countless others fail in this area, and as they come apart at the seams, so do their pursuits. We have to learn from those examples. More important, we have to refuse to let that happen to us. We have to adopt what the guys and I call *relentless integrity*. I'll explain what that means in a minute.

No matter what Go Big dream you're chasing, you're going to run into situations that challenge your standards and beliefs. And how you handle those situations will either prove or disprove your integrity. Failure in that area can destroy everything you've worked for. We believe the key to preventing that from happening is to lock down—beforehand—exactly what your standards are.

Let me give you an example. As our videos gained in popularity, we received lots of requests from the media. But in addition to those requests, various advertisers contacted us, wanting to pay us to support their products. While it would have been great to get paid, there was a problem. Both as a group of friends and as a business, we realized that partnering with particular companies would take us further from, not closer to, our goals. We recognize the opportunity we've been given to influence people younger than us, and throwing that away for money would be a horrible decision. Money is a powerful thing, and we'd be lying if we didn't admit we considered each offer. But saying no to those companies was the right thing to do. It built character in all of us, and it further established the type of integrity we want Dude Perfect to have: relentless integrity.

Relentless integrity means having standards that go well below the surface. It means taking real action and making hard choices, all based on values that matter to us. It means seeing those values as more important than money or fame or any other temporary thing offered to us.

People often ask us why we make the decisions we do, why

OTHER OFFERS

We also had a well-known magazine ask to write a feature about us. That article would have given us huge exposure to a new audience, but because of the magazine's risqué content, we declined. That's just not who we are. We've turned down TV show offers for the same reason. If it's not consistent with our values and beliefs, we're out. Simple as that.

we walk away from certain offers or care so much about integrity. Honestly, it's because of our faith in Jesus Christ. Years ago, each of us decided to live for God, not for ourselves. And when Dude Perfect started, we kept that approach. If we thought this life was all about us, sure, we'd take every offer that comes our way, make as much money as we can, and use this platform as a way to try to make ourselves feel cool. But that's not how we view life. God has given Dude Perfect this platform so we can help others and bring him glory in the process.

It's tough turning down some of these companies. I'm sure they think we're crazy, but we've seen too many people who, blinded by the spotlight and surrounded by loads of cash, chose to throw away everything they believed in. We don't want to end up that way. As great as money and fame sound, we'll pass. For us, it comes down to this: we feel blessed to have the platform we do, and we've each chosen to relentlessly pursue integrity because we want to protect the opportunity and influence we've been given.

On the flip side, sometimes you have to be willing to say yes—even when it costs you. We decided early in our journey that we were going to use Dude Perfect for a cause greater than ourselves. One of the ways we did this was by dedicating ourselves to giving back. And ever since then, though it has cost us plenty of money and time, we've made it a priority to live up to that promise.

In each of these examples, whether we said yes or no, we were able to do so because, when the moments of decision came, we had already pre-decided what to do. As a group, we determined early on the characteristics we wanted Dude Perfect to have, and we've made each decision with those characteristics as our filter. We've talked to a lot of people about this, people much smarter than us, people years down the road from where we are, people with scars, people desperate for us to avoid the same traps they fell into. And when it comes to decision making, every single person's advice boils down to this concept: Take a set of choices you've already made and let them become the lens you see through. This will take much of the emotion and temptation out of the decision-making process. If you do this, you'll keep your integrity intact and your dream on course. Consistently making the right decisions is hard, but as you and I have seen in the tabloids, recovering from poor decisions is much harder.

Our culture is saturated with people who have become successful and gone off the deep end. When we look at the tabloids, it's easy to assume these failures happened all at once. And while that's true on occasion, it's not the case the majority of the time.

I've always liked the saying "You are right now becoming the person you will one day be." The truth is that your life is made up of small decisions that build on each other to form the person others see you as. The way celebrities—and even others closer to our lives—morph into radically different people is by changing gradually change over time. Because life is made up of small decisions, each decision passes quickly, and it doesn't seem to be life changing. It doesn't get our attention because it's only a minor step.

Here's an example: Our sophomore year, Tyler grew out his hair. When I say that, some of you are picturing the original Justin Bieber length. Some of you are even picturing a solid Keith Urban length. Nope. Ty was rockin' a Troy Polamalu, Tom Brady, Jesus-length haircut. Now Ty didn't care how it looked, which was good, because, well, it wasn't exactly working

GO BIG TIP

Take a set of choices you've already made and let them become the lens you see through. This will take much of the emotion and temptation out of the decision-making process.

for him. Ask *him* about it, though, and he'll admit that it almost never crossed his mind. Day after day, he saw the slow progression in the mirror, and it never startled him. Truth is, he never really noticed how long it was . . . until it was out of control.

That's the way character works as well. Personal character issues are almost impossible to see in the mirror. That's why we have to be so careful about the decisions we make on a daily basis. If we're not careful, we'll wake up with the character equivalent of really long, shaggy hair, and no matter what Ty says, that's not a good thing.

It's also why we have to be so careful about who we surround ourselves with. The people you spend the majority of your time with will affect you one way or another. It's best to have people in our lives who will call us up to the standard we want to keep. You have to have friends who will tell you to cut your hair. Eventually the guys and I all told Ty that enough was enough. And if it hadn't been for us, Ty's hair might still be growing. And trust me—nobody wants that.

So if the key to making consistently good decisions is to base decisions on standards you've already chosen, then the most important thing you can do for your Go Big journey is to sit down and do just that. As soon as you possibly can, meet with your team, get out a sheet of paper, and list the characteristics you want to define your organization. Focus on the reputation you want your brand to have. Then, if there's a company you feel inspired by, identify and write down the qualities you appreciate about it. Finally, choose a company you never want to look like. Think about why you don't want to be like it—not just the surface reasons, but the underlying reasons as well—and put those negative characteristics on a list of things to avoid.

GO BIG TIP

Your life is made up of small decisions that build on each other to form the person others see you as.

If you're not running a business, if you're pursuing a dream on your own, create your list around personal characteristics, values you refuse to throw aside no matter what comes your way. You'll be able to consult this list every time you make a crucial decision. And for both the individual and the team, establish standards based on your personal beliefs as well. You won't be able to effectively help your team if you've allowed your group to take on a project you completely disagree with. When you trample on your personal integrity, you bring down your team's collective integrity. Don't do it; it doesn't help anyone.

Staying true to what we believe, guarding our standards, and protecting each of our Go Big dreams—these are all great reasons to value and prioritize integrity, but most of those decisions take place internally. There's also an external part to integrity, and it contributes more to your potential to relentlessly pursue your dream than any other idea we've talked about so far.

A great reputation and an attractive set of promises can only get you so far. The main thing your customers, your clients—whoever interacts with you—will care about is the experience they've had: the pleasantness, efficiency, fairness, and excellence you've brought to the table. This external aspect of integrity is all about how you deal with others. And here again I recommend relentless integrity.

We've all had horrible customer service experiences—unpleasant incidents so ridiculous that you roll your eyes just thinking about them. Each of those experiences was a colossal failure, a massive integrity breakdown on the part of the employee who "helped" you. Because of the way we're designed, it makes sense that we should be treated a certain way. That "certain way" makes up the external contents of relentless integrity.

It includes things like fairness, respect, not taking advantage of others, coming through on your commitments, and doing it all with excellence.

That's our goal every time we interact with someone. We try to stick to our promises—to let our yes be yes. We try to over-deliver on work we're hired to do. We try to give everyone we work with the respect they deserve, no matter what rung of the ladder they're on. We purposely avoid the term *fans* when referring to our viewers; we think having *fans* makes it sound like we're better than them, and that's not at all how we see it. We love talking to our viewers, and we try to respond to as many of them as possible. We try to give a hundred percent, even when we're tired or the situation is against us. We can't control our circumstances; we can only control our attitudes. Finally, we focus on staying humble, and we do that best by staying grateful.

The way you treat people is a crucial part of your Go Big journey, so take responsibility for the way both you and your team interact with others. Really own it.

It sounds harsh, but when you think about it, most of your competition is probably doing a poor job in this area. It's true; consistently doing these things is hard. That's why few organizations have outstanding, tell-your-friends-about-it customer service. The beautiful part: they're leaving the door wide open for you. So treat people right.

Your Go Big dream is far too important for you to let a lack of integrity bring you down. Guard your dream and your character by relentlessly pursing integrity. You'll separate yourself from the pack and keep your name out of the tabloids. That whole *any press is good press* thing? Um, false.

GO BIG TIP

Your Go Big dream is far too important for you to let a lack of integrity bring you down.

PART THREE

BLINK LATER

CHAPTER 8

THE SHOT SEEN 'ROUND THE WORLD

Life can change so quickly. For us, *quickly* was two hours.

It had been about a week since we released the "World's Longest Basketball Shot," and nothing had really happened. We'd put the video as our statuses on Facebook, tweeted about it, and e-mailed the link to a few television shows that had featured us before. I was all but convinced that the video wouldn't get off the ground—at least, that's what I thought before I got on the plane.

Coby and I were headed to North Carolina with our family to spend time with our grandmother, Mimi, and to help Catherine, our sister, check out a few colleges. When we boarded the plane from Houston to Raleigh, I was thinking about salted versus honey-roasted peanuts. When I got off, well, not so much.

During the flight my iPhone was on airplane mode, so when we landed, I turned it back on—nothing out of the ordinary.

MEET THE DUDES

Coby Cotton

Go Big Moment: Interview on stage in front of 14,000 at Catalyst conference

Go Big Dream: I would very much like to win Ninja Warrior.

My Best Kept Secret: Pretty huge fan of the old TV show *Supermarket Sweep*. . . . "Classic" doesn't say enough.

Favorite Shot: Field Goal Shot

DudePerfect.com

As my phone came back into service, though, it acted really weird. The screen flickered like crazy, it made this constant, buzzy chime like the speaker was broken, and it was shaking—not simply vibrating, but physically shaking. I thought it was broken. About twenty seconds later, the screen stopped flashing long enough for me to tell what was happening. Text messages, close to two hundred, and e-mails, closer to a thousand, had just flooded my phone. I pulled up the first text message as fast as I could and read, "Dude Perfect is on the front page of Yahoo!"

I turned to see Coby gaze up at me from three rows back. I looked back down at my phone and saw the next text message. It was from Tyler, and it said, "Two hours, two million views."

I laughed. No way was that true. But as I kept reading the texts, Tyler's message was confirmed over and over again. I waded through the aisle so Coby and I could celebrate. I'm sure everyone on the plane thought we were pathetic: identical twins high-fiving like we'd desperately missed each other during a two-hour flight.

Our parents and sister, who had sat together on the flight, beat us to the terminal and were waiting for us when we walked out of the tunnel. One look at their faces made it clear: they hadn't heard yet. One look at ours and they knew something was up. But hey, anyone could have guessed that. The way we were smiling, you didn't need motherly intuition to know we were excited. They rushed me to explain, and as I said the words out loud, it felt even stranger than reading them on my phone.

"Guys, our video's been on the front page of Yahoo! for two hours. Ty just texted us. It's got over two million views."

Our family had the same calm reaction we did. They freaked out.

The text messages were still pouring in, talking about our Yahoo! front-page status. Coby and I were dying to see it. Sitting down in an airport gate waiting area, I pulled out my computer and got online. I couldn't believe it. Right there, hanging out in the most featured spot on the front page, was our video. Smack dab in the center of the screen, Tyler stood holding a basketball at the top of Kyle Field. I can't blame people for clicking on it—it was pretty enticing. The headline read, "World's Longest Basketball Shot: Real or Fake?"

We didn't know it then, but Yahoo.com was at that time the single most visited website in the world, so being front and center on it was a huge deal. That moment was so surreal. I was looking at Yahoo!, a page I'd seen many times before, but at the same time, I, like millions of others across the globe, found myself clicking on our crazy video. I watched my best friends and me go nuts as we made a basketball shot from the top of Texas A&M's football stadium. In that moment, I felt like I was watching it for the first time. And, as if I hadn't actually been there that day, I remember thinking, *That looks like so much fun.* Then I saw myself run past the camera in celebration, and still sitting in the airport, I closed my eyes, went back to that moment, and laughed.

A few minutes later, I heard a familiar sound. At first I thought it was coming from Coby's computer. It wasn't. I looked across the aisle and saw a man smiling and then laughing as he watched on his laptop what we could clearly hear was our video. We heard the ball crash through the net and saw skeptical amazement sweep over his face. The moment was priceless and, again, surreal. For the first time, we saw someone stumble upon our video. As I was taking that in, I realized that moments like

Like most news websites, Yahoo.com moves the main story—in this case, ours—from the top spot to a secondary location, and then continually downward until it's either buried deeply or completely removed. Two hours of prime placement for our video turned into over two million views.

that, all across the world, were responsible for Yahoo!'s most-visited reputation.

Yahoo! being the prime real estate that it is, our video had to come off eventually. Consequently, in the mid-afternoon our video was taken off the front page. We'd seen two hours of coverage translate into over two million views. Together with its longer, but less prime placements throughout the day, we landed that night just past three million views. I called the guys throughout the day to laugh and exchange stories. For all of us, one thing was consistent. For the majority of the day, text messages and e-mails were coming in faster than we could read them.

Media requests had flooded our e-mail, and it seemed everyone wanted to learn more about the shot and about Dude Perfect in general. Television stations from all across the country—and even the world—requested immediate response, intent on being the first to scoop the story. We were shocked and humbled. We like to call what happened that day a *God thing*—something only God could have done. No matter what we called it, we were excited.

Needless to say, I found myself smiling a lot that week. Dude Perfect was everywhere, and the whole thing was ridiculous. Surely we weren't the only topic in the news, but at times that's what it felt like. Every news channel, it seemed, used the video as its hook into the show. An anchor would say, "Coming up later, you have absolutely got to see this." The whole clip would play, analysts would debate if it was real or not, and we would just laugh. As we'd seen with our other videos, the controversy fueled the hype more than anything else. When it showed up during ESPN's top ten plays, even NBA star Carmelo Anthony voiced his doubts. I can't really blame him, though. I was there, and part of me still doesn't believe it.

Everyone, including our families, was having a blast. For all of us, it was amazing to see how quickly the video spread. It was officially viral. In fact, that's the goal of every YouTube video—to go *viral.*

Before our first video hit the Tube, I had never heard that expression before. Someone had texted me saying, "Cory, I can't believe it—y'all are viral!" I texted back, "Dang. Do the rest of the guys know?" I've since learned that *viral* means that something—a video, a blog, a picture, a tweet, etc.—is spreading uncontrollably. It's incredible the type of saturation that viral content achieves.

For us, viral looks like this: if you Google "Dude Perfect," there are over 130 *million* search results, with relevant results coming up one hundred pages deep, Google's limit. It's weird every time I see it. It's hard to wrap my mind around the fact that our videos appear on websites and television shows all over the world. Could we have predicted our videos' global future? Of course not. The guys and I agree that only God could take something so crazy and do so much with it.

No one would deny that we live in a connected, fast-paced world. Especially not us, not now. That said, many people don't leverage this connectivity for what it's worth. We've experienced firsthand the speed and power of the connected world, and stressing that is the point of this chapter. One of our main desires for this book is to help you understand and seize the opportunities offered by the world we live in. For each of us to go big, we *have* to take advantage of the opportunities it offers us. In the previous chapters, we've flown through the first two

WILDERNESS WORK-STATIONS

That night we started our weeklong stay at our grandmother's Internet-free house. If we hadn't had our iPhones with us, we'd have been in trouble. But Steve Jobs would have been proud. Everywhere we went, we were multitasking, mobile-media workstations. We were a walking Apple commercial.

principles, Get Excited and Own It. This chapter is the beginning of the third principle, Blink Later. If you asked me to pick a favorite, I'd pick this one. It's *that* important to your Go Big journey. It's also really fun to talk about.

See, as we've lived the last three years in the fast lane, we've come to realize something crucial, something that's affected every aspect of our business, something that has become the foundation for this principle: in this increasingly fast-moving, technological world, your window of opportunity is too short to blink. The key to capitalizing on opportunities is to act now and blink later.

We began to realize this concept during the spread of our first video, but we didn't fully appreciate the scope of its importance until our "World's Longest Basketball Shot" went huge. Because of that, we couldn't help noticing that dreamers all around us were in desperate need of this principle.

With that in mind, I want to use the next few chapters to further explore this *Blink Later* idea. I'd like to begin by explaining a few of the many big-picture lessons we've learned from our experiences with the connected world.

I realize you probably don't need us to teach you about the Internet or to convince you that Facebook, YouTube, and Twitter are a big deal. Chances are, you're well-informed about what's going on. We thought the same thing before all this happened, and we considered ourselves pretty tech-savvy. But having experienced what we have, we feel like we've stepped into a whole new world. The simple fact is that our understanding of the connected world has changed immensely. It's significantly deeper than it used to be, and I know we'd be holding out on you if I didn't share what we've learned.

GO BIG TIP

In this increasingly fast-moving, technological world, your window of opportunity is too short to blink. Act now—blink later.

So for just a minute, I'm going to help broaden your opinion of the connected world by giving you some behind-the-scenes information about how viral our "World's Longest Basketball Shot" was. If you're anything like us, this will blow your mind.

First of all, our video's viral status makes it obvious that a whole lot of people watched it in a very short amount of time. So what kind of numbers are we talking about here? Well, in a little less than two hours, the video received over two and a half million views. Let's put those numbers into perspective.

The seating capacity for the new Dallas Cowboys Stadium— the largest NFL stadium—maxes out at 100,000 occupants, a load only reached for an event like the Super Bowl. Implication: twenty-five Cowboys Stadiums full of people, all stacked on top of each other, all packed to the Super Bowl brim, watched our video in less than two hours. Picture every single person in every single seat watching us shoot, swish, and celebrate—all on their laptops, desktops, and smartphones. Because that's what happened.

Those numbers are insane. That's a rate of 1.25 million views per hour, 20,833 views per minute, 347 views per second, and 34 real people choosing to watch a real video every tenth of a second. I don't know about you, but that's hard to wrap my mind around.

What we didn't realize at first was the other piece to this puzzle. For a video to be seen that quickly by that many people, the viewing had to take place, well, everywhere. We can study the demographics information on each of our YouTube videos, and when we look back at this one, the global breadth of this video is astounding. US. UK. Australia. Japan. New Zealand. Germany. The list goes on and on.

What's the point of this information? When this video exploded to the far ends of the earth, so did the content. That seems obvious, but think about the effects that had for us as a business, as a brand. Back in the day, it took companies a good ten to fifteen years to establish a global brand presence. Our Dude Perfect brand literally went global in less than two hours. How? A shot seen 'round the world.

When most people hear that our brand "went global" that quickly, the tendency is to ask whether it really took hold. It's easy to assume this was a quick in, quick out scenario, that the brand recognition didn't *stick* in those far-reached areas. I think that's a fair question. From what we've experienced, this is how I'll answer it: the overseas demand for our content (for TV show licensing purposes) and for our merchandise (clothes, hats, bumper stickers, etc.) rivals that of the United States, falling behind by only about 20 percent. Countries like Germany, Japan, Australia, China, New Zealand, and many areas of the UK—just to name a few—have thrilled us with their interest in our content.

Our global relationship with television shows, media outlets, viewers, and customers has, without a doubt, been one of the most exciting parts of this entire process. Did we pursue each of these relationships and continue to invest in these situations? Yes. Did almost all of these connections come from this one video? Yes, they did.

Here's the incredible news. If you have something compelling to offer, the connected world offers you avenues to distribute your vision farther and faster than ever before. To better demonstrate that fact, let me end this chapter with a success story that has nothing to do with us.

In 2008, Andrew Mason launched a company called Groupon. The brand's basic idea is brilliant. By partnering with local businesses, Groupon offers its online audience daily, city-specific deals on food, shopping, and entertainment. By advertising on Facebook and Google, the idea went viral. By fully leveraging the connected world around them, Groupon's business range exploded. Before I knew it, the company I'd heard about only months ago was airing its own prime-time commercial during the Super Bowl.

In a press release issued in January 2011, Groupon described the growth the company experienced in 2010: "Groupon expanded from 1 to 35 countries, launched in almost 500 new markets, and grew subscribers by 2,500%, from 2 million to over 50 million." Putting those numbers into perspective, *Forbes* magazine labeled Groupon the fastest-growing company ever. So what's Groupon worth? Currently $4.75 *billion*.

By using the connected world, Groupon quickly spread its idea, created an online community of buyers, and sustained a growth pace that's made it the fastest-growing company in history. The coolest part is that we, as Go Big dreamers, have the same opportunity that Andrew Mason had. Take it from us (and Groupon): your compelling idea, message, cause, or talent is just waiting to be strapped to the connected world's rocket-propelling potential. And as the next chapter will show, that type of momentum can open up opportunities you never thought possible.

GO BIG TIP

If you have something compelling to offer, the connected world offers you avenues to distribute your vision farther and faster than ever before.

CHAPTER 9
HIT THE SAC

If you want to know what blinking later looks like in real life, you're about to see it. This chapter is a case study of our fast-paced Sacramento adventure—a play-by-play tutorial in blinking later. As you see instances where we made quick decisions and capitalized on opportunities, think about ways you might apply this concept to your own dream. Focus on the areas you tend to hesitate in, areas you find unnerving, and areas with unknowns surrounding you. As you'll see, those are some aspects of your Go Big dream that can benefit most from a Blink Later mind-set.

A week after the Kyle Field shot went huge, e-mails were still pouring in. It was hard to keep them straight—and even harder to decide who to respond to first. The majority of conversations involved media and news outlets seeking a story. But every once in a while, someone reached out to us with a game-changing idea, something that expanded Dude Perfect's horizons. *That* was a benefit of the connected world we hadn't seen coming.

TIP #1

The decisions you make set the course for your brand, so remember that whenever you're making quick decisions about opportunities that come your way.

PLANES & PANDAS

I said we packed our bags, but one was actually a box; the Dude Perfect Panda's not allowed to fly coach. (We'll explain more about our mascot in chapter 14.) Coby tried to explain the box's fluffy contents to the lady at the bag-check station, but she was thoroughly confused— it must have been her first time checking a panda.

TIP #2

Don't force others to blink at the opportunity to give exposure to your brand. Make it easy for them to promote what you have to offer. Make a highlight video, a PowerPoint presentation, a website, etc.—anything that clearly and attractively lays out your brand's appeal.

While we *had* guessed at huge potential for growth among our viewers and followers, we hadn't predicted the opportunity potential that would come from that video's enormous exposure. One opportunity in particular commanded our undivided attention.

The e-mail asked if we would be interested in flying out to Sacramento, California, to film some videos to hype up Tyreke Evans's campaign for 2009–2010 NBA Rookie of the Year. The first time I read that, I took a deep breath. This offer meant a lot of things. It meant a high-profile athlete wanted to align himself with us. It meant we were being asked to represent a brand other than our own. It meant others were taking notice. But saying yes also meant stepping out of our comfort zone, working with someone besides ourselves, and partnering in a Rookie of the Year campaign—something no one had ever done before. The choice we made was crucial. It set the tone for the type of brand we wanted to be.

So what did we say? We said yes.

The timing of the trip worked best for Cody, Tyler, Coby, and me, so when the day came, we packed our bags and drove to the airport. After an uneventful flight, our plane touched down in weather much cooler than what we'd left behind in Texas. We walked through the terminal gate and stepped onto the escalator toward luggage claim. While riding down, we saw a flat-screen TV that said, "Welcome to Sacramento, Home of Tyreke Evans & the Sacramento Kings." We looked at each other and smiled.

Outside the terminal, our driver pulled up, introduced himself, and helped us load our stuff. It was already late in the afternoon when we pulled up to our hotel, so we went inside and got ready for the night ahead. Later that evening we were set to film some shots inside Arco Arena, home of the Sacramento Kings. But before that, we got to see something else inside those doors. It was game night for the Sacramento Kings, and we had tickets.

Thirty minutes before tip-off, our driver brought us to the arena and walked with us through the staff entrance. We were greeted with VIP passes to hang around our necks. With the passes, we toured the arena and ate in the staff's pregame dining room. In certain places, there were "All Access Only" signs above the doorways. With our VIP passes hanging around our necks, those signs might as well have read, "Please Enter, Dude Perfect."

But even before we'd experienced the power of the pass, we glanced down at our tickets: Kings Row 1, Seats 1–4, also known as the four best seats in the house. We were blown away. We knew the Kings were hooking us up with tickets, but we never thought we'd sit courtside.

We were escorted toward the court through a special, floor-level tunnel entrance. Soon, under the bright lights and surrounded by the crowd, we felt like we were on the Kings' team. We walked up onto the slightly raised court and took our prime-time seats near the baseline goal. It was unbelievable. Finally, as we were sitting down, I noticed that the guy a couple of seats from us looked familiar. Soon enough, I'd remember who he was, and we'd be shaking hands.

As we took in the grandeur of the moment, a staff member introduced us to the Kings' production MC. He informed us that halfway through the second quarter, he'd be showing a highlight video of our shots and introducing us live on the stadium's big screen. We looked at each other and laughed. *All right, then. Let's do this.*

NETWORKING

Cody is incredible at making connections. He networks with everyone he meets and always takes the opportunity to explain our Dude Perfect vision. Often it's his networking connections that provide us access to the incredible facilities we use. And this situation was no exception.

TIP #3

Predetermine your big goals so you can be on the lookout for opportunities to actually reach them.

Right before halftime, the lights went dark and our Dude Perfect highlight video appeared on the big screen. The crowd really enjoyed it. When the lights came back on, we were already standing up with the MC. He briefly explained the Kings' plan to link us to Evans's Rookie of the Year campaign and thanked us for our time, and we sat down to the sound of more applause.

As if we hadn't been honored enough, at halftime a lady on staff offered us passes to the VIP room for refreshments during the downtime. Thanking her, we took them.

The refreshment room was great, as was the rest of the game. We enjoyed every moment of the fast-paced play, as well as the unusual star treatment, and as the game wrapped up, we assumed our extra attention was nearing an end as well. Wrong again.

First of all, Cody, as he does so well, met the people a few seats down from us, one being the man who had looked so familiar to me earlier. After shaking his hand and trading business cards, Cody introduced the rest of us to the mayor of Sacramento, Kevin Johnson. Mayor Johnson is the former star point guard of the Phoenix Suns, a player I'd watched growing up.

One of the goals for our trip to Sacramento was to shoot from the balcony of the California capitol building. So when we met Mayor Kevin Johnson, we knew he had the authority to help us reach that goal. Sitting back down in our seats, we turned over the mayor's business card, and thanks to Cody, we saw the name and number for the capitol building's head of security, as well as the mayor's assurance that he'd help us make the shot happen.

Often, blinking later means making quick decisions. In this case, however, blinking later meant networking and capitalizing on the contacts we made. Not only had Cody been intentional

TIP #4

Networking is huge! It's quick, effective, and worth the time . . . every time.

TIP #5

Never blink at the opportunity to thank your supporters.

AFTER THE GAME

enough to meet the mayor and share with him our desire to use the capitol building, but he also used the contacts and generosity of the mayor to our advantage. Cody didn't hesitate. He was bold, and he had the capitol building to show for it.

As you can imagine, we were getting a little delirious from how incredible the night had already been. But the craziest part was still to come. As soon as the game ended, people from the stands loudly rushed the court. We assumed they were coming to get Evans's autograph or maybe a picture with Brandon Roy. But the NBA players walked past, and little attention was directed toward them. To our surprise, these people were looking at us. Purple-clad Sacramento fans of all ages crowded around the court, trying to get our attention. Those who did asked us to autograph their Kings gear: shirts, noisemakers, hats, and even shoes. They asked us to take pictures with them, and when their phones didn't take the pictures just right, they'd ask if we'd please take another.

We were floored. Over a hundred people in that stadium waited almost an hour for a picture and autograph from four of the guys they'd apparently seen on their computer screens. We weren't used to that, so it was fun—and strange at the same time. But even though we were a little confused, we didn't hesitate. Though the interactions were fairly short, we wanted everyone who met us to know how much we appreciated them. Not often having an opportunity to interact that closely with our viewers, we tried to capitalize on the moments we had. We gratefully stayed, talked, signed, and posed until we'd met everyone who lingered.

Sacramento had really rolled out a red carpet for us. But before we went back to our hotel that night, we had a few plans

TIP #6

A *blinker* spends too much time on small shots—the ones he or she knows are possible. A Blink Later person goes for the big shots early on. Don't waste too much of your time in the "possible" zone. Reach for big goals. When you grab hold of them, you'll be glad you did.

TIP #7

Hesitation is a leading cause of blinking. Don't become a statistic. Like Tyler, take a deep breath and move on.

TIP #8

Part of blinking later is allowing others the opportunity to step up and help you. Even if it seems unrealistic at the time, ask others to help you with your biggest goals. They might just surprise you with a mascot trampoline.

of our own to accomplish, plans to give back to the Kings, to film some shots for Tyreke's campaign.

Before we'd seen inside the arena, we were excited about some of the things we might be able to do. But seeing it in person inspired us even more. As Kings fans headed out, our tip-off was underway. We had all night to film shots inside an NBA arena. Tired of watching other people shoot, we gave Reke a good-game high five and got right to work.

In preparing for our time there, we'd asked the Kings' staff about everything from climbing in the stands to climbing in the rafters. We weren't exactly sure which of our planned shots we'd end up doing, but we almost preferred it that way. We love making quick, Blink Later shot decisions—capitalizing on the inspiration surrounding us.

After a few smaller shots on the court left us bored, we went straight for one of our biggest ideas: the catwalk shot. Tyler rode with a few basketballs up an elevator, and I stayed on the court to help rebound what would surely be a lot of misses. The Kings staff had warned us about only one thing with this shot, and that was to please not break the shot clock directly above the goal's backboard. With that in mind, Tyler took a ball, aimed, and tossed it off the catwalk toward the target below. The ball carried a lot farther than he'd guessed. Coming in hot, it went straight for the shot clock. Seconds later, the ball flew over the goal, missing the shot clock by inches. No doubt about it, Tyler's stomach had dropped as quickly as the basketball. But narrowly avoiding disaster, Ty regained his composure and continued the attempts. Five minutes later, he'd been super close but still had come up short. His shots had hit off the rim and both sides of the backboard, but because of the speed, height, and angle of the shot, there was almost no margin for error.

Unwilling to accept no for an answer, Ty began his second round of attempts. By this time, I'd ridden up the elevator to see the shot from his angle. From probably the highest up I'd ever been, Tyler was aiming at a minuscule target far below us. And then it happened. Not two minutes after I walked up there, Ty sent a missile at the goal below, and a few seconds of hang time later, the ball rocketed off the glass and through the net to the court below. It was awesome. We couldn't believe it, and our celebration proved it. I gave Ty a high-fiving bro hug, and we celebrated one of the crazier shots we'd taken. We knew it would look sweet on camera, and we were right.

With one awesome shot in the books, we got a surge of energy. It was late, but we didn't care. We were ready for something really big. As if perfectly timed, we got some incredible news. Earlier we had asked about borrowing a mascot trampoline, and just then someone brought us the Kings' official stunt trampoline. If you've never tried one, let me tell you, it only takes one jump to understand why someone might want to be a full-time mascot.

We messed around with dunking from farther and farther distances and even did a flip onto the blue safety mat in front of us. Then Ty had an idea, one that turned out to be the biggest shot of our series for Tyreke. For this shot, we placed the trampoline at the free throw line and faced it toward the goal on the far end of the court.

On his fifth attempt, Ty dribbled up to the trampoline, jumped into a front flip, and hurled the ball soccer-style over his head. Everyone in the arena collectively shook their heads

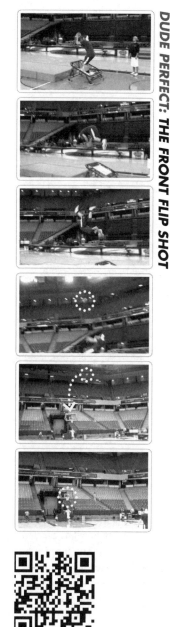

DUDE PERFECT: THE FRONT FLIP SHOT

DudePerfect.com

as the ball swished through the net on the other side. After the shared moment of disbelief, we all went berserk. The shot was unheard of. It takes a ridiculous amount of strength to even get the ball that distance, and Ty had just swished it in only a handful of tries.

The alarm clocks weren't our best friends the next morning, but we knew we had a packed day ahead. The night before, Cody had talked things over with Vito, head of security for the state capitol building, and in the morning, he finalized a time for us to film there. We were still amazed at the shots we'd gotten the night before, and to follow all that with an opportunity to shoot from California's capitol building was unbelievable.

We laughed as passersby tilted their heads at the unusual scene: four college guys rolling a basketball goal up to one of the most breathtaking places we've ever seen. We set the goal forty yards from the building. Cody and I stayed outside while Coby and Tyler entered the building, basketballs in hand. When they appeared, Cody and I couldn't help but laugh. Standing on the beautiful balcony between intricately carved columns, Coby and Tyler were each holding a basketball. It was official: we'd seen it all.

By the time we were ready to begin, a solid crowd had formed. It turns out no one had set up a basketball goal outside the capitol before. No doubt there were a lot of unknowns surrounding that shot. But just like everything else that weekend, we blinked later, not getting hung up on those unknowns, plowing through them with quick decision-making. For example, the capitol building's security guards were understandably worried about the safety of the tourists walking around outside. Understanding their concern, we

PICTURE THIS

The sun bathes the capitol in a warm glow. The musical bubbling of a fountain welcomes you. A manicured lawn, the kind picnic baskets dream about, lies beside you. The flowers are almost too bright to be real. And there you are—rolling up with your basketball goal to one of the most breathtaking places you've ever seen.

TIP #9

To move quickly, you're going to have to cooperate with the authorities around you. Remember, there are already enough obstacles in your path; don't work against the people you need on your side.

worked in unison with their personnel to make tourists aware of the flying basketball zone.

Having secured a fixed area, I gave Tyler the thumbs-up to begin. Tyler told future viewers on the other side of YouTube, "This is the Capitol of California Shot." Then, from the balcony of a landmark, Ty let it fly. Despite strong winds and the pressure of having an audience, Ty nailed the shot in about fifteen minutes. Throughout his attempts, the crowd was very encouraging, so when he made it, they were just as excited as we were. My favorite part of the video is seeing the full view of the capitol at the end of the shot. It shows how epic the scene was. We loved it. We had one more shot left to film, but as we rolled the goal away from its spot, we laughed and reminded ourselves that we were walking in front of California's state capitol building—with a basketball goal.

We arrived back at the hotel, the location for our last shot of the weekend, what would soon be known as "The Hotel Drop Shot." The very first time we walked in the hotel, we had thought of this idea. We wanted to place a goal inside the lobby and drop a shot from the interior balcony of the top floor, the eighth story. We knew what we were asking sounded crazy: do a shot inside a functioning hotel? But fortunately for us, the hotel's owner was also part owner of the Kings and wanted to help Tyreke Evans any way he could. Trying to be as careful as possible, we again worked with necessary decision makers, in this case the hotel managers, to clear the area of people and anything else they preferred we not hit with a basketball.

With the area roped off and the goal in place, Ty, Cody, and I rode the elevator all the way up, peeked over the edge, and looked down at what seemed like a very small basketball goal.

DudePerfect.com

But we were determined to prevent our hesitations from stopping us on this one. I grabbed a ball, spun it on my finger, held my arm out over the edge, and with a silent *Please, Jesus, don't let me break the hotel* prayer, I let the ball drop—all the way down. The ball narrowly missed the target. The three of us looked at each other and smiled. This was awesome. A few tries later, with the ball spinning and adrenaline flowing strong, I peered over the edge, took my aim, and let it drop. It felt good. . . . It looked good. . . . *Swish!*

We'd accomplished what we came for. We'd filmed some unbelievable shots, shots we could use to help promote Tyreke's campaign. Thankful for a successful weekend, we packed our bags and headed to the airport. California had been great to us, and yet again, we felt blessed.

As the months passed, we soon realized how important that weekend was for us. By agreeing to do something we'd never done before, by aligning ourselves with Tyreke and his campaign, we enhanced our brand's portfolio significantly. We'll explain more about that later, but our Blink Later instincts had been correct—it was crucial to do something different, to break the mold. By working on this project, we branched out and expanded our brand in a way we never could have done had we simply stayed where we were. We saw an opportunity and capitalized on it. That's the definition of Blink Later.

As you continue on your Go Big journey, make sure you don't get stuck in a pattern that seems to be working just fine. In this fast-paced world, the moment we coast, we actually slide backward. Resist the urge to stay put. Force yourself to dive into the unknown. You'll be glad you did.

DudePerfect.com

CHAPTER 10
BREAKING POINT

How can an idea be so good and so bad at the same time?

A couple of our guys go to a church in Dallas, Texas, called Prestonwood Baptist. It's a really big church. The tallest point on the building is a cross tower, peaking at around 150 feet. We love big stuff, so when one of the pastors suggested we do a shot from the cross tower, our eyes more than lit up. We planned the date for the shot, and when the time rolled around, we made our way to Dallas and set up shop in front of the tower. Oh, and did I mention it was nighttime? Yeah, not only did we plan the highest shot we'd ever attempted, we wanted to do it at night. In order to see the ball, we set up some of the church's industrial lights.

It took a while to figure out how Tyler was going to throw the ball off the roof of this tower. See, the actual roof is recessed about seven or eight feet below the walls of the tower. Picture yourself standing inside a tall cylinder, unable to see out of the top. *That's* the situation we were in, and the solution was a little sketchy. We leaned and attached a ladder to the front side of the wall and strapped Tyler to the leaning ladder. With the ladder's help, Tyler could see out the top of the cylinder and down to the tiny goal 150 feet below. Finally, at about ten o'clock at night, we were ready to start.

The bright industrial lights lit up the pitch-black scene. We were excited to see how cool this would look on camera. We'd been wanting to do this shot for a while, so when it was finally go-time, we couldn't wait. We'd asked a few people to help us, and one of the guys that was up top in the tower handed Ty the first ball. Ty announced, "This is the Cross Tower Shot," coiled back his arm, and released the ball. As the ball flew toward the ground, the previously quiet night was interrupted by the clanging of Tyler's ladder against the inside of the tower wall. Four, almost five seconds passed as the ball soared toward the goal. Finally, the ball landed five or six feet away from the target—not bad at all for a first try.

But throwing several more shots, Ty realized that, being as high as he was, the wind was making it hard to maintain his consistency. It seemed like almost every other shot was blown in a different direction at the last second. Ty kept plugging away, but before we knew it, our two bags of basketballs were empty and it was time to refill. The best return system we could come up with was a rope that the up-top guys used to pull the balls up the center of the tower. On their way up, the bags of basketballs had to fit through a narrow channel in the center of the tower, surrounded by a circular staircase that stretched almost the entire height of the tower. The bags would bump into or get caught by the metal stairs. It was frustrating, and it took forever.

Finally, it was time for round two. Twenty minutes passed,

and as the shots added up, so did the rebounds. Down below, Cody and I tried to cheer Tyler on, but you could tell we weren't super pleased with this shot. It wasn't that the shot wasn't cool; it was extremely cool. It was that Tyler wasn't getting very close at all, which was unlike him. Round two finished, then round three, and with each passing set of basketballs, the night got blacker and our eyelids got heavier. We couldn't believe it was taking this long. It was midnight, and we'd been at it for two hours now, a full hour longer than any shot before. But the misery was just beginning.

Rounds four, five, six, and seven came and went, and as they did, the group's morale plummeted until it was scraping the floor. With every miss, Cody and I sprinted to snag the ball in the parking lot, also trying to get back to the goal in time to celebrate if Ty were to make it on his next shot. It was exhausting, and after each round, while we waited for the guys to pull the basketballs up the tower, Cody and I lay down on the concrete, desperate for a break. When it was time for Tyler to shoot again, we'd slowly pull ourselves off the now almost-comfortable-feeling concrete and return to sprinting after misses.

It was a little after one o'clock, and with the three-hour mark in our rearview mirror, we weren't sure what would be worse: quitting after this much effort or continuing to waste time attempting something that might never happen. We couldn't stand to let this one go; we knew it was possible. Tyler had hit the backboard a couple of times, but out of the probably two hundred shots so far, the odds of success looked downright awful.

Utterly exhausted, we took a much-needed Whataburger break, delivered by Tyler's mom and girlfriend. No one wanted to talk. No one wanted to say the words *let's quit* or *let's call it a*

MEET THE DUDES
Cody Jones

Go Big Moment: Launching our very own iPhone game

Go Big Dream: Have children that beat the other DP guys' kids at sports

My Best Kept Secret: I accidentally shot an undercover cop with a water gun.

Favorite Shot: Garrett's missed layup at the end of my "Through the Plane Shot"

DudePerfect.com

OUR TOUGHEST SHOT

In most of our experiences, the shooter's attempts would get closer and closer, but Tyler's were almost getting worse. The wind whipped, taking the ball in unpredictable paths, and the ball was almost impossible to aim. The nighttime added its own set of problems. Not only were the industrial lights in Ty's eyes, but the darkness drastically affected his depth perception.

night, but if someone had, I doubt the rest would have argued. Think about the worst all-nighter you ever pulled in school. Now add a Chicago Marathon to it. That's how we felt. We were physically and emotionally drained. We were mad at the world. We were mad at each other. We were mad at the cross tower. And above all, we were mad at each and every stubborn basketball that refused to go in.

✦ ✦ ✦

The Cross Tower Shot describes our Dude Perfect journey almost too well. So far you've read about the seemingly endless good news and the quick successes. But that's not the whole story.

As we were in the first few minutes of the Cross Tower Shot, we were initially excited about everything happening in Dude Perfect. We'd started the group for fun. We'd had some early success. We saw great potential for our group. We kept making videos that kept doing well.

Our routine was working pretty well. But there was a problem, and similar to Tyler launching shot after shot off the tower, everyone felt the pressure build. There was always stuff to do, and we're not talking about basketball shots. Most of it revolved around the business end of things. E-mails, conference calls, project proposals, legal issues, and contract negotiations—it was a lot. And as time went on, the workload kept increasing. Before we knew it, this group we'd started for fun was blazing past the hobby category. Dude Perfect began to take serious time to manage.

Honestly, the responsibilities had become overwhelming. More than twenty tasks had to be managed on a weekly, if not daily, basis. And with only a small team of guys, all in college, all dealing with life outside of Dude Perfect, the weight was discouraging.

As any company will tell you, certain people at certain times naturally end up carrying a larger load than others. And while in our experience this was no one's fault, it added another layer of frustration to the group dynamic. None of us really had time to pursue this crazy dream. We were staying up studying for a math exam, then staying up past that to respond to urgent e-mails. We were editing videos while our friends went to the movies. The college life was evident in the fun of the videos but not in the work behind them.

We'd begun to chase a dream that, like the Cross Tower Shot, had a ton of potential. But as we kept going bigger and bigger, we realized the process was going to be a lot harder than we'd thought. In the past, we'd been able to see more clearly what was ahead of us, but with everything going as quickly as it was, we didn't know how to move forward. No one had ever done what we were doing, so no one else's opinion could really help us solve the problems we were facing.

Besides the lack of clarity for our future, there were other factors at work. Similar to the leaning ladder Tyler had to throw from, our plans were constantly shifting, and no matter how well we tried to schedule our time, we had to make sacrifices in other areas of our lives in order to move forward with our Dude Perfect vision. The unpredictability of the wind showed more clearly in our world. There was no way to tell what was going to happen next. The fluidity of our Internet-based job made it tough to rely on, and as we got closer to graduating, we had to decide if we were going to keep pursuing something that, at that time, wasn't putting much bread on the table. Finally, like the shot dragging deep into the night, we were exhausted. The fun was gone. Burnout had set in. Whatever we were doing, we were tired of it. No one announced it; no one had to. We'd hit our breaking point. We had to make a decision.

So, over the course of about a week, we entered now-or-never mode. On one hand, everything we'd worked for over the last couple of years was on thin ice, and for all of us, that was difficult to think about. On the other hand, we had run smack-dab into a wall of disagreement with each of our best friends. It's one thing to have a tough conversation with someone you don't care about. But this was conflict and tension between guys who wanted our friendship to survive the conversation.

As tiresome as it was, we knew the only way to make any progress was to talk it through. So we did just that. For hours and hours, we talked. To make things worse, we weren't all living in the same city, so we had to have most of these conversations on the phone.

Having multiple guys involved in this process made it almost impossible to agree on anything. We disagreed about the future of Dude Perfect—its potential, both as a YouTube group and as a brand. There was conflict about our individual responsibilities, what types of videos we should release, and whether we should even *be* a company. We couldn't agree on anything. There were long, back-and-forth discussions lasting deep into the night—just thinking about it makes me tired.

At the end of this, we didn't know what sounded worse: continuing to chase a dream that might eventually fail or choosing to give up on a dream that might eventually succeed. *That* was the main question. And it was time to decide.

GO BIG TIP

It's never pleasant, but sometimes the only way to make progress is to talk through a difficult situation.

✦   ✦   ✦

Around 1:30 a.m. on the night of the Cross Tower Shot, Tyler and I had what was the deciding conversation, the defining moment for the night. He asked me what I wanted to do, and though everything in me wanted to quit, I couldn't say it. We'd never even thought about quitting a shot before this, and even though the Cross Tower Shot had turned out to be more dif-ficult than anything before it, we both knew we shouldn't *choose* to walk away. If we quit right then, we would be making a permanent change to our philosophy. We'd be saying, "Shoot for the impossible—until you think it might actually be impos-sible. Then quit."

The other part—the harder part for me—was thinking about quitting on each other. Tyler had thrown hundreds of balls that night, and even though none of them had gone in yet, I was moments away from basically looking him in the eyes and say-ing, "You can't do it; I don't believe in you." I knew Tyler would never say that to me, and I wasn't about to say that to him. We're too much of a team to give up on each other. People we cared about had helped us get this project in the works, and those people had given their time to help us that night. Giving up now would have made their efforts count for nothing, and we couldn't do that. My body wanted to fall asleep on the concrete, but my team needed to finish strong. We came to a group deci-sion to push on. We were determined to keep fighting.

I wish I could say our decision to move forward made the shot a little easier, but it didn't. The wind still whipped, the dark-ness still surrounded, and the ladder still wobbled. The basket-balls hoisted up the fifteen-story tower didn't get any lighter.

NOW OR NEVER

If you're wondering why we didn't just quit for the night and try again another day, this shot was a fairly large-scale process, involving way more than just us. Because it was unlikely that we could have this opportunity again, we had to make our decision as if we were walking away from this shot for good.

And the concrete parking lot didn't get any softer. Everything was still difficult.

But almost two full hours later, a little over five hours since we'd begun the night's adventure, Tyler sent a ball hurling off the ladder, out into the darkness, down through the wind and into the net below—*swish*. Our celebration that night—or morning—will probably never be matched. Our cheers weren't those of pure excitement like normal. They were a mixture of perseverance, relief, victory, and appreciation for the decision to move forward. Because of everything that had gone into it, that swish was more fulfilling than any before it.

Most important, and I actually mean this, that moment grew our group's character—especially our perseverance—in a way that few other events could have. It was one of the worst, and best, nights of our lives.

✦ ✦ ✦

Wanting to quit a shot is one thing; wanting to end our group is another. We'd come to the end of a weeklong, now-or-never process, and after much debate, we landed on the only two available options:

1. Continue to pursue Dude Perfect in a Go Big, full-steam-ahead, non-hobby way.
2. Give up.

That's how we saw our options shaking out. We agreed we couldn't force Dude Perfect into an only fun, only safe, only

DudePerfect.com

small, only hobby category. Therefore, our only other option was to walk away. But as you know, we didn't do that. We chose to keep Dude Perfect alive.

That horrible season in our company's life has turned out to be one of the most valuable experiences we've had. Making it through the problems we faced, working through the tension we had, and protecting our friendships in the process has drawn us closer as a group and inspired us more toward our dream. The thing I've noticed most is that, like the tower shot, our group constantly looks back to that breaking point for encouragement. Knowing that we made it through such a tension-filled situation gives us strength to deal with the other battles we face.

The Cross Tower Shot was a pretty miserable experience. And our breaking point was the worst week of my life. So how did we make it through, and how can you do so when your company is in a similar situation? We've got some answers to that question.

First of all, we believe that when a team wants to quit, there is a certain type of person who, despite the frustrations around him or her, brings encouragement to the surface. This type of person naturally sees through the fog and into the clear sky on the other side. This type of person is a *visionary*. In our group, we're split almost down the middle—*visionaries* and *down-to-earths*. Both personalities are necessary. The visionaries provide huge goals to aim for, and the down-to-earths help bring balance. They make sure the group doesn't spend all its money, for example, or plan way too many events. Visionaries have a tendency to overestimate, while down-to-earths underestimate.

But in an all-hope-is-lost scenario like the one our group

faced, visionaries are key to moving forward. Visionaries lift people's eyes past the current situation, inspire others to press on, and remind them to never give up.

And *that* is our second point. We *refused* to quit. As a group, we were struggling in lots of areas, but no matter how much tension we had to work through, quitting wasn't a legitimate option. It went against everything we believed in, both as a group and as individuals. What we learned is that, no matter how hard it gets, you are never done until you actually quit.

There's one final factor that was crucial to our decision: God. When we first started the group, we could tell God was using it. And from early on, we decided to pray, both as a team and as individuals, about major group decisions. This was, obviously, a major group decision. And as we prayed about what we should do, we all felt like God wasn't done with Dude Perfect yet. We decided that as long as God wanted us to keep going, we'd follow his lead. And we're so glad we did.

So when you face difficulties—and you will—look to the visionaries in your life for encouragement, keep a never-give-up attitude, and if you're up for it, pray. You *can* make it through difficult times, and as we've seen, you can grow from the process. In this section, we've been talking about the Blink Later principle. Well, in this case, there's no way around it; hardships make you blink. The key is to not blink for long. Whether it's a night of filming or a week of talking on the phone, don't waste time. Push through the problems you face. It's not easy, but trust us: your dream is worth the fight.

GO BIG TIP

No matter how hard it gets, you are never done until you actually quit.

CHAPTER 11

THE AIRPLANE SHOT

Remember Tyreke? So did the judges. Reke won 2009–2010 NBA Rookie of the Year, and he truly deserved it. We were pumped for him and happy that we had the chance to help him out in even a small way. We'll be the first to admit that Tyreke probably had Rookie of the Year locked up without Dude Perfect, but for fun, let's pretend his winning had something to do with us.

Regardless, the campaign was as successful for us as it was for Tyreke. As the videos went viral, the media talked about our affiliation with Tyreke, the Sacramento Kings, and consequently the NBA. Though some media personalities made fun of the campaign, most congratulated it, applauding our alignment with an up-and-coming star. With the word out that we'd done a successful marketing campaign representing someone other than ourselves, we began to receive offers from other interested parties. In April, we got one that gave our Go Big mind-set wings—literally.

MEET THE DUDES

Tyler Nathan Toney (TNT)

Go Big Moment: Shooting 3 raccoons with one bow-and-arrow shot

Go Big Dream: Set longest dunk record by getting shot out of a cannon

My Best Kept Secret: I have a secret, musically inclined alter ego on YouTube. Search "RappaT."

Favorite Shot: Airplane Shot—second try

DudePerfect.com

In a very professional e-mail, the Leo Burnett ad agency asked if we were interested in filming something for its client, GMC. The agency's goal was to launch an online campaign connecting Dude Perfect with GMC's brand-new pickup truck, the Sierra Denali HD. We spoke with agency representatives on the phone, bounced ideas off each other, and eventually landed on a sweet concept: "GMC Heavy Duty Pickup Games." The connection between what we do and what the truck does was great. We loved the pitch. It sounded like a great match for us, and we couldn't wait to see it through.

The next step was to come up with potential shots, but in order to do that, we had to know where we were going to film. Backyard? Football stadium? Tyler's ranch? In one of our conference call conversations, we could hear the smiles in their voices as the agency reps told us, "Nope. Austin, Texas." We understood their enthusiasm better when they asked us if we could think of any cool shots using an open pasture, a rock quarry, a high-rise construction site, and an airplane. As we huddled around the phone, we laughed and said what they knew we'd say: "Um, yeah."

We felt like a new world of possibilities had just opened up to us. We were given a much larger canvas than ever before. For the first time, we were asked to paint some of the biggest shots we could imagine. The feeling was surreal, truly epic. We were artists who'd been handed colors we never knew existed.

Fast-forward a few months—to game time. We all arrived in Austin. As we met in the hotel lobby, the excitement was undeniable. We were about to spend three days hanging out with our best friends and filming some of the coolest stuff ever. Getting several busy guys on the same schedule is almost impossible, so all of us being there was impressive. While hanging out in the lobby, we realized this was the first time we would all film together since the very first video almost a full year before. Thinking about that, we were more excited than ever.

The next day our ride arrived at 5:00 a.m., so of course we woke up at 4:55. We college guys hadn't seen those numbers on a clock in a long time. We rolled out of bed, down the stairs, and out the front door. Cody, a professional sleeper, was last to the van.

We met our driver, John, who took awesome care of us all weekend, and we headed out. An hour, a banana, and a sunrise later, we pulled up to our destination, a pasture cleverly hidden past miles of highway and winding dirt roads lined with tall trees and bushes. We knew about the shots we were supposed to do, and we knew we couldn't find our way out of that pasture if you paid us. But we never expected what we saw.

As the van turned the corner, we found ourselves in a green field surrounded by trees. Filling the space between the tall tree walls, two things caught our eyes. First, there were cars, and lots of them. As early as it was, we thought we were going to be the only ones there, but at least fifteen vans, cars, and trucks were scattered in the field. Wondering where all their passengers were, I then saw the second thing: a large, white tent even bigger than the ones you see at weddings.

We walked inside and were greeted by who we quickly found out was the Leo Burnett team. We'd only spoken on the phone before this, so it was fun to finally put faces with their voices. Then we noticed something to our left, something glowing. Recently awakened, the sun had sneaked quietly through the doorway, its beams now resting on a couple of tables piled high with muffins, bagels, breakfast burritos, fruits, and drinks—breakfast fit for a king. Since most of us had late-starting college classes, we didn't usually eat breakfast. But staring at the enticing feast in front of us, we thought, to be fair, we should let breakfast be the most important meal of the day at least once that year. Sitting down with a couple of plates each, we did our best to make up for lost time.

To the right of the glowing food tables was the crew of about thirty to thirty-five people. Until we saw them, the idea that there would be a crew had barely crossed our minds. We knew we didn't have to bring our own video equipment—and by "video equipment" I mean our one digital camera that we set on video mode whenever it's go-time. But we never would have guessed there'd be a thirty-five-person team ready to help us.

After meeting the crew and eating enough breakfast for the year, we asked Andi, the head producer, about the game plan for the day. She answered with the words we'd been waiting months to hear: "This morning, we're filming the airplane shot."

Pause. If you've already seen the video, you know exactly what she's talking about. If not, let me back up and point out the other thing we gawked at inside the massive tent. GMC had prepared for this day by renting a Piper Cub crop duster. It was a beautiful matte yellow with a smooth black stripe down the middle, and it looked like it wanted to be all over the Internet.

We went out to the field expecting to be moments away from filming, but we quickly learned we were playing by different rules now. Because this was a professional production, the hit-record-and-go style we were used to wasn't going to cut it here. First Ethan, the sound guy, hooked each of us up to a wireless mic. Then we moved on to getting "greeked," taping

COMPETITIVE DOWNTIME

While one of us was getting miked or greeked, the rest played a game Coby and I invented a long time ago. The goal is to pass the ball back and forth by making fluid one-handed catches and behind-the-back throws. Though difficult with two guys, adding a couple of others makes it extra tough. And we love extra tough.

over any shoe or clothing logos to prevent having to pay royalties. During this long process, we realized how unbelievably dominated by the culture we were. We were apparently keeping Nike, Polo, and Texas A&M in business.

It was now time for us to unload the goal from the truck. Reading that probably doesn't sound like a big deal, but at the time, because we hadn't seen the truck in person yet, it was awesome. Parked way out in the field, with a flatbed trailer attached to it, was the coolest truck we'd ever seen, the first ever GMC Sierra Denali Heavy Duty. Two guys were in charge of keeping it clean and safe, and they opened up the hood and showed us the serial number, 000000004. Of the 2011 line, there were only *four* of these trucks in the world, and we were looking at one of them.

After we unloaded the goal and put it in place, it was time to do what no one had ever done before, what we'd come to a cow field in the middle of nowhere to do: make a basketball shot from an airplane.

The weight of the situation was undeniable. The pressure was really on, for a few reasons in particular. For one thing, because we usually film our own videos, there is rarely anyone besides us on-site. Also, we use one or, if we're feeling ambitious, two cameras; looking around us that morning, we saw seven high-definition, "oh, hey, there's a drop of water on a blade of grass" cameras. Finally, doing a shot from a plane had been by far the most frequently requested shot idea we'd received, so the months of buildup from countless viewers, e-mails, and our own conquering nature made this moment extremely powerful.

The plane's engine fired up, and life again was moving as fast as the plane's propeller. As much as we trusted the pilot and

TRICK SHOOTING 101

When filming a commercial for a new truck line, avoid locking the keys inside, especially when only four of those trucks have been made.

the plane, we only had Tyler, our resident daredevil, take to the skies. Excited and unfazed, Captain Clutch put on his pilot-style headset, got a few final high fives from us, and climbed into the yellow aircraft.

The pilot put the plane in gear, and we laughed as Cody yelled, "We love you, bro!" The plane rolled through the field, slowly at first, until it had enough speed to take off. After a turn much wider than our anticipation could stand, the plane, with Ty and a couple of basketballs inside, was a hundred yards away, staring us in the face.

We smiled as we heard the producer's excited voice. "Plane Shot: take 1!"

More than a hundred feet in the air, the craft screamed toward us. We couldn't contain ourselves. We were all yelling at the same time. We were freaking out.

Seventy yards. Sixty. Fifty. The engine was deafening. Forty. Thirty. He was almost over us now. Twenty yards. The ball was in his hands. Ten yards. "Tyler! Drop it! Now!" Release . . . the ball fell fast. We swung our heads to the right. . . .

Nothing, not even close. Forty, maybe fifty yards past the goal.

The screaming stopped. We stood there for a moment, silent. It felt like someone had punched us in the stomach with a plane. We tried not to care; we'd missed before. But this felt different. Ty wasn't even close to *being close*.

It hit us that we'd be out there till dark, and suddenly the day felt long. The fun we were having only minutes earlier seemed distant, and when five minutes later it was time to try again, we were all faking smiles. After circling round, the plane pointed its nose toward the goal and came in for another attempt.

Behind us we heard a disheartened voice say, "Plane Shot: take 2."

Passion leaking quickly, we yelled a less-than-convincing "Go Tyler, yay." The plane was fifty yards away. Forty. The engine was still piercing. Thirty. We waved our signaling hands in the air, earlier this time. Twenty. "Drop it, Ty! Now!" He let it go. Like before, it was a laser, but this time it was coming toward us . . . no, toward the goal! We swung our heads with the ball, and it was in the net.

Our world exploded. We were running into each other, going who knows where as fast and as loud as possible. We were in shock, freaking out, triumphant.

"He made it!"

"Boom!"

We knew we weren't supposed to look at the camera, but at some point, we just had to look at the crew. They, too, were absolutely losing it. There wasn't another way to handle the situation. There was hugging and jumping, and jumping while hugging. There was laughing, screaming, open-jawed disbelief, and the biggest smiles I'd ever seen. Headsets were flying everywhere. It was emotion unleashed. It was unbelievable.

After what seemed like an endless celebration, we all began to catch our breath. People were saying real words again, words that could be heard without yelling. Words like, "Who wants to see the video? Everyone to the tent!"

Obviously we were dying to see it. And when we did, it didn't feel real. We'd been there, and it still looked fake. We all talked about how no one was going to believe it for a second. Like watching film after a big game, we rewound the magical moment over and over again.

CONFUSED CELEBRATION

After watching the plane shot a few times, the producer pointed something out.

"You know how after a game-winner there's always that one guy who's so happy he just runs the opposite direction? Well, watch Sean."

Replaying the video again, we all died laughing. Sure enough, Sean sprinted away from the group the moment the shot went in. Priceless.

About this time, Tyler landed. We'd been having our own private party without the guest of honor! Running toward the plane we could see him smile and hold out a triumphant fist. As we congratulated the hero, he just laughed.

In that shining moment, he was thinking what we all were: *Did that really just happen?*

Despite the emotional roller coaster it put us through, the Airplane Shot was an enormous success. Beforehand we didn't know exactly how it would turn out, or if it was even possible, but looking back, we're so glad we didn't blink. During the shot-planning process, we could have easily settled on a simpler shot, one with a 100 percent success rate, but we didn't. We told GMC that we wanted to go big. The plane idea surfaced, and despite our doubts and hesitations, we went for it. GMC gave us the opportunity, and we took it to the skies.

What we've learned is that often the key to landing truly big opportunities is to shift our mind-set. Here's the deal. The human brain is a wonderful thing. It lets us come up with incredible dreams, Go Big dreams, and even lets us imagine what life might be like if they came true. But then, out of nowhere, it turns on us and talks us out of the very idea it came up with only moments before. We can talk ourselves out of anything, and that's great when it's a fourth or fifth straight episode of *24*. But it's tragic when it's a Go Big dream.

Join us as we change the way we think. See, as you pursue your Go Big dream, you'll find yourself coming up with Go Big ideas—like a plane shot. As those ideas come along, your natural tendency, like ours, is to blink, to take in the moment and think long and hard about it. That's normal, but as we both know, it can really hold us back. We live in an increasingly fast-

GO BIG TIP

Don't talk yourself out of a Go Big idea by sitting on it for too long. Again, don't blink. Act.

moving world, and with a *regular* mind-set, one of two things is bound to happen: You'll either talk yourself out of an idea, or worse, someone else will beat you to it—stamping their name, instead of yours, all over it. The way we see it, neither of those options is okay.

Instead, when you have a legit Go Big moment, resist the urge to overthink it, to *blink*. Right now, reading this, you might assume our point is "don't think." Wrong. As we explained in chapter 3, we believe you should always get good advice and be wise with your decisions. What we're really saying is don't talk yourself out of perfectly good ideas by sitting on them for too long. Take some college guys' simple advice. Don't blink your way through life and regret it later. Instead, do what we did with the Airplane Shot: blink later.

And let's be honest, what we did was absolutely crazy. I mean, we tried to make a shot out of an airplane! The fact that it worked didn't really make it any less crazy; it just made us and the rest of the crew even more excited about the incredible shots left on the schedule. So we took that excitement with us as we walked toward the van, ready to move on to the next site. Climbing in, we were still laughing about how terrible Ty's first attempt had been. His first shot was closer to a cow than to the goal—and no, the cows weren't anywhere near the goal. Laughing himself, Ty agreed, yet cleverly asked for a show of hands from anyone else who shoots 50 percent from an airplane.

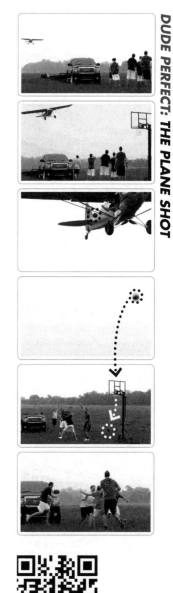

CHAPTER 12

PLANE TO PINEAPPLE

So what do you do after you shoot from a plane? How do you follow that? Apparently you head toward town to shoot through a moving train. That was the plan, at least, and as you can imagine, we were pumped. As we arrived at the train yard and walked toward the train we'd be using, a thought occurred to me: *How do you rent out a train station?*

"Excuse me, ma'am, we'd like to use the train today to film this basketball shot, so it'd be really great if you could secure the tracks for us. . . . Oh, yes, just for today. Will that work? Great, I really appreciate it."

Well, however it happened, it happened. We had our own train.

With cameras set and each of us still miked, the second shot of the day was underway. The mission was to shoot the ball through an open but moving boxcar into the goal on the other side of the tracks. The boxcar's sliding door was only six

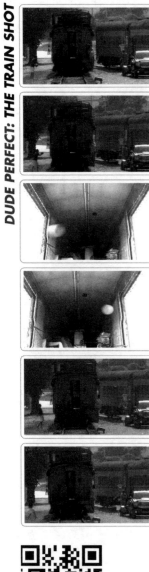

DUDE PERFECT: THE TRAIN SHOT

DudePerfect.com

feet across, and when the train was up to speed, it seemed a lot smaller than that.

Feeling game-time ready, one of us tried to tackle the task. Key word: *tried*. Here at Dude Perfect, we care about each other greatly, so to fully protect the identity of the failed shooter, I'll simply refer to him as "Coby," a mystery man who looks frighteningly similar to me—in fact, he could be my twin. Coby consistently waited too long to shoot, and with the boxcar flying down the tracks, the inside of the boxcar kept swallowing the basketball. We tried to coach him through the "choke," reminding him to shoot *before* he could see the car's opening, but he couldn't make himself pull the trigger any earlier. Some things in life are just hard to watch. Miss after miss, he'd act confused and surprised, and we'd support him by dying laughing.

Imagine for a moment that you're a baseball coach. It's the first inning, and twenty-six pitches into the game, your pitcher hasn't thrown a single strike yet. What would you do?

I'll tell you what we did. After watching that train go back and forth more times than a model train collector could stand, we pulled our twin pitcher and put Sean on the mound instead. And after a couple of warm-up misses of his own, Sean made the adjustment and nailed it.

Before we left the train yard, Captain Clutch wanted a try at the shot that had proved so difficult all afternoon. With nothing to lose, the crew sent the train down the tracks one final time. The boxcar fast approaching, Ty released the ball, cleared the opening, and banked it in! Going crazy, we celebrated with the guy who had proved his focus more than ever that day. With Tyler shooting 50 percent from a plane and 100 percent through a moving train, the crew probably thought he was a god. Though obviously not the case, there's no doubt he'd had a killer day. As Coby and Sean shook their heads at Tyler, we loaded into the van—just another day at the office.

The rest of the weekend was just as successful. The next day we traveled to a quarry and filmed a shot with a bulldozer, a shot involving a crane, and a shot jumping from a small cliff into the water below. On the last day, we ended the week by going into the heart of the city to an unfinished high-rise building. First, Coby redeemed himself by launching a shot from the tenth story of the high-rise to the top of a parking garage across the street. We followed that with a shot from the ground to the highest goal we've ever seen, a third shot bouncing from inside the high-rise down to a suspended I-beam, and finally the last one from a metal container suspended more than one hundred feet in the air down through ten consecutive basketball goals welded together and attached to the side of the building. The shots were epic, filming them was a blast, and they turned out great.

As you've watched these multiple-shot videos of ours, you've probably noticed a trend: the best shots are spread out. We do that on purpose. We want to keep the world's ADD audience as engaged as possible throughout the whole thing. Then, at the end of every video, we finish with the biggest, baddest grand finale shot, the one we're most excited about, the one we hope will leave your jaw on the floor. The final shot is the epitome of a Go Big moment, and it's the type of shot we aim for every time we think up a project.

But here's the straight-up truth, a reality we can't deny no matter how desperately our Go Big mentality wants to: not every one of our shots is going to be a "plane shot." We want

GOOD DAY, BAD DAY

For Tyler, that was a very good day. So to keep him humble, I'd like to reveal one of Tyler's bad days. No basketball here. Let's just say this video involves a skateboard and a roof.

DudePerfect.com

Not every idea will be a plane shot, but don't let that stop you. Blink later— focus on keeping your content fresh.

it to be, we try for it to be, but often we finish a weekend of shooting with only one "plane shot" on film.

All the Go Big dreamers out there—including us—have to understand that that's okay. Whenever a Go Big dreamer accomplishes a plane shot, the first question we all hear is, "How do you top that?" And while that's a healthy thought for a dreamer to have every once in a while, it's also the kind of thought that will drive you insane. It's the type of thought that can make you *blink*—bringing your momentum to a screeching halt. Instead of blinking, instead of letting the desire to go bigger and bigger with each shot overwhelm us into doing nothing, we've decided to do something different.

Instead of focusing all our energy on the biggest, baddest finale shot, we make sure to save some brainstorming power for the supporting cast of shots. The key to filling in the gaps between our "plane shots" is to frame the other ones with creativity. Remember, our shots and your projects don't always have to be insanely big and spectacular. Sometimes, engaging content is as simple as fresh content. Frame your ideas in unusual settings with unexpected people, and paint your ideas in a light that will catch anyone's eye.

Our GMC shots weren't all out of an airplane. We used unexpected scenery, multiple goals, moving targets, and changes of perspective to create engaging content. For you and for us, every idea won't be a plane shot, but don't let that truth stop you. Blink later—focus on keeping your content fresh. That's what will allow it to be relevant in this fast-moving, connected world. Finally, remember that even though every idea won't produce the same jaw-dropping reaction as your plane shots, every idea can and should be carried through with excellence.

A Go Big mind-set is as much about producing excellence as anything else. Excellence is always our overarching goal, our real focus every time we go to work.

Our GMC project included an incredible plane finale combined with an array of other excellent shots, and we were extremely proud of it. It contained some of the coolest shots we've ever done, and we were able to pull off such fresh-idea shots because of the awesome crew we worked with. Remember, *that* was a brand-new experience for us; we'd always made our own videos. So for a few minutes here, I want to share some thoughts about what it was like to work with a production crew.

A few things stand out as particularly memorable. First of all, it was great to work with a group of people who cared as much about excellence as we do. The people on the film crew were professionals who took their jobs seriously. Remember what we talked about in the Get Excited section? These people fit that description. They were excited to be out there filming with us, and that excitement helped fuel us for the work that we had to do. But they also didn't take themselves so seriously that they couldn't have a good time. They were professionals, to be sure, but their commitment to excellence didn't outlaw fun. In fact, their excitement and openness to fun fostered an environment where creativity and excellence were able to run wild.

As far as the experience goes, what we've talked most about since that time is what it was like to be constantly miked. If you've ever been miked for a long period of time, then you know what this feels like. If not, picture our experience as if it were your own.

You arrive on set with five of your best friends, and from moment one, you have a hidden microphone attached to you.

DudePerfect.com

Whatever you or any of your friends say can be heard by at least eight people that you met only minutes before. Hearing your every word are, among others, producers, cameramen, and sound controllers, most of whom are huddled in a tent slightly off set, looking at the various camera angles on monitors in front of them.

There are definitely pros and cons to this. On the downside, you're affected by the simple knowledge that every conversation you have, from normal to pointless, from inside jokes to stupid arguments, is being heard. Now obviously there's a difference between *hearing* and *listening*, and the professionals hearing us were certainly not always *listening* to us. We knew this because, well, remember the pro side to the mics? To us first-timers, our mics often doubled as one-way walkie-talkies. So as the weekend went along and we got to know the crew better, we had plenty of fun with our baby-monitor connection to the headset-wearing people around us.

For example, during the downtime on set, our favorite pastime was messing with Ethan, the head sound guy. Part of his job was to make sure our sound levels stayed correct, so he was glued to his headset and forced to listen to us more than anyone else was. Knowing this, we had super fun one-way conversations with Ethan. When we couldn't see him, we did our best to "entertain" him. We told him stories. We occasionally sang. And when we *could* see him, we would test his ability to focus by questioning him during moments when he was supposed to be paying close attention to the producers.

We have to hand it to him; his track record was pretty phenomenal. I think we broke through a couple of times, but he gave a solid performance. Ethan was a stud; he put up with a lot and was a good sport about it. Despite our best efforts to fluster him, Ethan did his job and did his job well. We were able to depend on him, knowing that he was doing phenomenal work. And best of all, his professional demeanor and good humor kept the rest of us at ease and enabled us to perform at the highest possible level.

Besides being miked constantly, we've talked often about another aspect of the trip. During our time on set, we were treated very well, more or less like movie stars. We understood that the crew was used to working with actors and others accustomed to that type of treatment, but since it wasn't something we were used to, we barely knew what to do with it.

For example, when we filmed the cliff shot, we each rotated through until Cody eventually nailed it. We would jump off, laser the ball toward the goal, land in the cold water, surface, find out it hadn't quite gone in, swim to the side, climb over rocks and up a ladder, and end up back where we started. The route was a little tiring and we were soaking wet, but that was fine with us; we were doing what we love to do. Here's what was so new to us: once we reached the top of the ladder, someone was there with a dry towel, a warm blanket, a tasty brownie, and rich hot chocolate. As you can imagine, that was kind of awesome.

After the first day, the guys and I discussed this whole idea. Yes, we were in front of the camera, but we didn't want to be guys who acted like we deserved special treatment. The truth, we decided, was that we didn't feel *entitled* at all. We felt blessed to even be in a situation like this. The tricky part was that it was literally some people's job to make sure we were doing okay while we were in their care. A perfect example is Donna.

FUN WITH ETHAN

We sang Ethan classics like "Sweet Ethan of Mine." ("Ethan's got eyes of the bluest skies, as if they thought of rain. I'd hate to look into those eyes and see an ounce of pain.")

Donna was in charge of the food. Remember the kingly breakfast we enjoyed that first morning? Donna. She catered meals and passed out snacks, and somehow she always seemed to pop up at the perfect times. During a blazing hot day—bam! Cool lemonade and fresh-cut pineapple. Coming out of that cold water—bam! Hot chocolate. After a long, tiring shoot— bam! The best sandwiches you've ever had. We joke that whatever you pictured in your mind as the perfect food for that moment, all you had to do was turn around and Donna was standing there holding it. She was awesome, and we appreciated every single thing she did for us. We think there's at least a 37 percent chance she was an angel.

We eventually decided the best way to handle the star treatment was to simply be appreciative. While some people may take that type of kindness for granted, we wanted to do the opposite. See, real movie stars go home to their mansions; we go back to college. Generally speaking, your college years are one of the most low-maintenance seasons of life, and our experience is certainly no exception. The way we see it, if it's someone's job to keep us hydrated on a hot day, we don't have to refuse the water; we just need to make sure we're as thankful on the outside as we are on the inside.

As you confidently pursue your Go Big vision, your interactions with those around you will set you on one of two roads. The first is the *I'm so caught up in my own story I can't even see you standing there* road. This road, as we've all seen, is a disaster waiting to happen. Actors who freak out on set and athletes who cheat in order to win—both are examples of people whose goals and viewpoints involve only their own glory. Don't choose this road.

The second is the *grateful* road. The person on this path is the award winner whose acceptance speech is so self-deflecting and others-honoring that those in the crowd realize the truth: it's not all about the person in the spotlight. By spreading credit where it is rightly due, a grateful speech builds into relationships. An entitled speech does only damage.

Remember, the answer is humility, not arrogance. No matter how successful you become, don't be the type of person who acts entitled to others' good treatment of you. The people who act that way have allowed themselves to get caught up in their own stories.

Don't ignore the people around you. If you do, you'll look back on those relational opportunities as ones you blinked at and missed rather than valued. Instead, be appreciative of others—on the outside as well as on the inside. Take every opportunity to affirm the role, no matter how small, that someone else plays in your Go Big pursuits. Remember, Blink Later means taking advantage of every moment you have, and that includes your interactions with others. It doesn't mean moving so fast that you blow others off or don't thank them. Our philosophy is simple: take advantage of opportunities, not people.

One of our favorite memories of the GMC weekend was working as a team with the crew. Everyone there did their part to make that weekend possible, and when it came time to shoot, everyone else wanted us to make the shots as badly as we did. We all had the same hours, all put on sunscreen, and all celebrated when a shot was successful. It was a team effort—plane to pineapple.

GO BIG TIP

Take every opportunity to affirm the role, no matter how small, that someone else plays in your Go Big pursuits. Blinking later means taking advantage of opportunities, not people.

CHAPTER 13
FULL SPEED AHEAD

I've heard it said, "Don't tweet it before you eat it." In other words, don't let the whole world know you're *about* to enjoy a piping hot, mouth-watering Chick-fil-A sandwich before you even take your first bite. When you do that—some would say—you pre-experience the sandwich online instead of actually experiencing it in real life.

I'm not quite sure how much truth there is to that, but the way I see it, the fact that an idea like that exists at all says something about our world. Our world is far more "instantaneous" than it's ever been before. In fact, I believe that we live in an almost *pre*-instant world.

That sounds weird, but think about it this way. Picture a fourteen-year-old girl on her way to the mall. Sitting in the backseat of her mom's car, smartphone in hand, she tweets on Twitter and posts on Facebook, "Heading to the mall. . . . Can't wait for Hollister and chocolate ice cream with my girls!"

Whether she knows it or not, I believe there's something

driving this girl—as well as the rest of the similarly minded, connected world—to update the universe on what she's *about* to do. I'm sure you've heard people say our culture is one of *instant gratification*, and while that's clearly true, I actually think our technological culture is transitioning toward *pre-instant gratification*. That's what compels the girl to ping her whole connected world with what she's about to do.

Some would argue that the girl's actions are compelled by her desire to *feel* connected to others. And while I agree that plays a role, I think it's deeper than that. The girl heading to the mall posted, "Can't wait for . . ." That type of statement is revealing. The truth is, she literally *can't wait* to hang out with her friends at the mall, so much so that she has to find some level of pre-instant gratification before the actual event. She gets this by pinging all her friends and waiting for a response from them. People fulfill this desire by commenting on her post with things like, "I love Hollister!" or, "Chocolate ice cream is my absolute favorite!" or, "I wish I didn't have homework. I would come!"

These responses not only give the girl a sense of connectedness to the outside world; they give her a significant level of pre-enjoyment related to the mall trip itself. She is able to pre-enjoy her trip through the comments, and even jealousy, in response to her original post.

What does this have to do with your Go Big dream? Why am I telling you this? There's one main reason: whether you're selling to a fourteen-year-old girl or not, this is your audience.

Because *instant* isn't quick enough for your audience anymore, you have to realize that you're dealing with extremely fast-paced expectations. And since this is the pace your audience expects, you need to market your content, products, and services with that reality in mind. Whether we like it or not, at the end of the day, our Go Big dreams will succeed or fail based on how desirable what we're selling is to an insanely fast-paced, connected world.

Here's something else you need to realize: your organization is a legitimate brand. Maybe you believe that; maybe you don't. We didn't necessarily think about Dude Perfect as a brand until we started working alongside other campaigns, first with Tyreke, then with GMC. Our young "brand" feelings were confirmed, however, with the positive results of the GMC campaign.

As I explained earlier, the main purpose of the campaign was to create viral hype around the launch of the Sierra Denali HD pickup truck. That said, we knew that if we created absolutely outstanding content, there was also a chance it might appear in print through *ESPN The Magazine* or on television as some type of GMC commercial.

And since the airplane shot was such a smash success, we were pumped to hear that we were going to get our wish. Print? Yes. TV commercial? Yes as well. As if that weren't enough good news, we were quickly informed that since GMC was the lead sponsor for that year's NBA Finals, our commercial spot was going to air during the actual games!

As you can imagine, we were thrilled out of our minds. I can't tell you how much of an out-of-body experience it was to watch the Lakers play the Celtics in an epic, old-school, seven-game championship matchup and see our faces come on the screen during a fourth-quarter, prime-time commercial break.

Apart from our obvious approval of the campaign's results, GMC stated that the campaign was one of their most successful

GO BIG TIP

At the end of the day, our Go Big dreams will succeed or fail based on how desirable what we're selling is to an insanely fast-paced, connected world.

of all time, garnering over *one billion* impressions worldwide. That number—a combination of the commercial's airings during the NBA Finals and during the FIFA World Cup, as well as all the videos' online traffic—reinforced the humbling reality that the length of our Dude Perfect reach was growing, and growing quickly. So much, in fact, that on the heels of this campaign, *Advertising Age* listed Dude Perfect as one of the top ten YouTube brands that current companies wanted to associate themselves with. Whether we'd *felt* it before or not, it was official—we were a brand.

As we all know, however, that advertising article didn't *make* us into a brand; it *recognized* us as one. And while that was nice for us to hear, what we want you to understand is that, with or without official recognition, your organization *is* a legitimate brand.

The important question isn't whether or not your organization is a brand, but what steps does your brand need to take to best reach the fast-paced, connected audience in front of you?

That's where we think the Blink Later principle can help. We want to give you three practical, *don't wait another second* steps to do just that—to best position your organization, your brand, in front of this audience. We are fully aware that the people holding this book are at all different stages of business. That said, some of these concepts will apply to you more than others do, but whether you're a business tycoon or an entrepreneurial beginner, we believe these Blink Later application points will be helpful. The most important thing to remember is that the Blink Later principle, like the other four Go Big principles, is most effective when treated as a mind-set. If you put the connected-world situations you encounter through the Blink

GO BIG TIP

With or without official recognition, your organization *is* a legitimate brand.

Later filter, we believe you will be well equipped to make fast, wise decisions that ultimately benefit your brand.

1. KEEP YOUR BRAND FRESH AND RELEVANT

Your audience has ADD. Period. If you don't treat them like that, they will move on before you even know they're there. What that means is that you need to constantly introduce fresh ideas and fresh content into your system. For us, that means constantly working on new videos and trying to put them out as often as possible. First, we have to focus on coming up with fresh, new, innovative ideas that relentlessly raise the bar for our videos. We can't project a Go Big mentality and not regularly be looking for ways to raise our game. It just wouldn't make sense. The same goes for you. If you want others to be impressed with what you have to offer, you have to consistently look for innovative ways to raise the level of excellence that people are used to seeing from you.

But here's the other side of the coin. If we don't release videos quickly enough for our viewers, Dude Perfect will lose its relevancy in their lives. It's like your favorite television series. When the season is on, it's relevant to your life. But once the season is over, the show loses its impact on you, and you forget about it. The most successful YouTubers out there release content on a regular basis. Their viewers notice it, they come to expect it, and eventually they come to depend on it. Whether you're releasing a video or not, the key here is to keep your brand on the minds of your audience. And from what we've seen, *that's* what's so powerful about social media. With Facebook and Twitter, you can keep your audience constantly plugged in to what's going on inside your brand.

The goal for any brand is to create a strong bond between the audience and the brand itself. We believe the key to doing this is giving your audience something to grab hold of. For us, it's our Go Big attitude. By constantly projecting our Go Big mentality, we allow our viewers an opportunity to grab hold of that idea themselves. If people identify with our Go Big slogan, they will have ultimately identified with us as well.

Create an intentional bond with your audience, and then keep them connected to your brand. Remember, when it comes to engaging and maintaining the attention of an audience, fresh equals new; relevant equals often.

2. LOCK DOWN YOUR REAL ESTATE

Since you want your audience to get to know your brand, you have to give them ways and places to do that. If you haven't done it yet, we cannot stress to you enough the importance of securing your brand's online real estate. Start by grabbing Twitter, Facebook, and YouTube account names that, if at all possible, match your brand name. You will need to attach e-mail addresses to most of these accounts, so if you don't have a business e-mail yet, try getting YourBrandName@gmail.com—that way you will have a semiprofessional e-mail address to attach to these various online accounts. Blink later; launch your social networking platforms right now. Set this book down and do it. We don't mind. Why? Because every day that you wait, you are missing out on potential followers.

If you don't know where to start, create a Facebook fan page for your organization. When someone "likes" your page, all of your updates to that page will be sent to that person's news feed, essentially keeping you in constant contact with that person. Now here's our favorite part. If Billy "likes" your page, then all of Billy's friends will be notified that Billy did that, and lots of his curious friends will click on your page to see if they want to "like" it too. Before you know it, your Fan page will grow, often exponentially. The key is to start. What we've noticed is that the YouTubers with the largest followings are almost always the ones who have been around the longest. Get going, and watch your audience gain in number and momentum.

Now, and this is probably the most important thing, you need to lock down your domain, your URL, your website. If you've never done that, just go to a website like NetworkSolutions.com and search for the domain names you would like the most, and once you find a good one, buy it. A domain name is usually around ten dollars a year, if it's available. As I'm sure you're aware, this is your most important online real estate, so taking care of this quickly is absolutely crucial for your brand.

3. CAPITALIZE ON OPPORTUNITIES

The core of the Blink Later principle revolves around capitalizing on opportunities. If you are going to make your shot count in the connected world, you have to take advantage of the opportunities in your path, both the ones you discover and the ones that present themselves to you. A lot of people miss out on opportunities because they freeze at the decision-making point. As a Blink Later person, you absolutely cannot do that. We've found that the best way to make quick, wise decisions is to

CHOOSING A DOMAIN

You want people to be able to find your website, so the best domain names are ones that are easy to remember. Aim for short, easy-to-spell words, and if you can, choose .com, .org, or .net as your extension—in that order.

DESIGNING A WEBSITE

There are lots of ways to design a website, but unless you know code, you'll want to use a program like iWeb for the Mac or an online site like WordPress.com, both of which allow you to customize different premade, cool-looking templates.

pre-decide how you want to handle certain things. Remember the chapter about integrity? Remember how we talked about setting a foundation of values and boundaries that you can then base future decisions on? This is the same idea. In order to make quick, wise decisions when opportunities arise, you need establish guidelines ahead of time, guidelines you can return to as you rapidly evaluate the opportunities in front of you. If you decide what your brand's major goals, boundaries, and danger points are, you'll be able to quickly evaluate future decisions against that predetermined filter.

Another part of capitalizing on opportunities is managing your time well so that projects don't fall through the cracks. For example, March Madness is always the craziest part of our year, for obvious reasons. This past year, for example, we had more projects on our plate than we knew what to do with. Instead of turning down valuable opportunities, however, we found a way to juggle and maintain each project through to its completion. It can be chaotic at times, but taking advantage of busy situations now may eventually give you more of a cushion in the long run. You never know what will or will not happen in the future. All you can do is take care of what's in front of you.

Last thing I'll say about this: whether you're working on one project or juggling a few at a time, the best way to capitalize on an opportunity is to knock it out of the park. There are too many people out there selling mediocre products and services. Don't be one of them. If you strive for excellence in everything you do, people will notice. Even though we're a young company, we've seen that professionals around us are impressed with the way we do business. We may be a crazy group of college

BUILD YOUR BRAND

A colleague from the television industry complimented us, saying, "I'm continually impressed with the way Dude Perfect does business—the smart ways in which you build your brand."

students, but for us, excellence is one of the most integral parts of our Go Big approach.

How else could we end this section than with a quote about the king of this Blink Later concept, Coca-Cola. Crowned the best global brand of 2010, Coca-Cola is undoubtedly the best of the best. I could go on and on praising the company's incredible efforts, but instead, I'll let Interbrand—the world's leading brand consultancy—brag on the carbonated red-and-white brand that has captured the hearts and wallets of the world:

> *Coca-Cola gets almost everything right. Its brand promise of fun, freedom, spirit and refreshment resonates the world over and it excels at keeping the brand fresh and always evolving*—all this, while also maintaining the nostalgia that reinforces customers' deep connection to the brand. *For such a large brand,* it operates quickly, flexibly and innovatively, *tailoring itself to local markets without tarnishing its legacy. This includes different flavor profiles in each country and shrewd distribution models in fast-developing world markets (for example, carts in India).* It has adapted quickly to social media, *with 11 million fans on Facebook and 96,385 followers on Twitter as of August 2010.* (emphasis added)

PART FOUR

INSPIRE
OTHERS

CHAPTER 14
PANDAMONIUM

There is an unexplainable cool factor to having a mascot. Every great team has one. The Anaheim Ducks' Wild Wing, the Energizer Bunny, the Geico Gecko, Tony the Tiger—all super cool, and all representing a certain brand. Once it dawned on us that we were mascot-less, suddenly nothing else mattered.

I don't know how other people do it, but we went straight to the Internet. We looked up cool mascot costumes, anything we could think of, and pictured them in our minds. The Dude Perfect Turtle? Monkey? Bulldog? All incredibly lame. We wanted something that screamed awesome, and these didn't. Finally, we found him, and like meeting a best friend for the first time, we knew we'd be hanging out again soon. There he was, on some obscure website, shining in all his glory: the Dude Perfect Panda.

Everyone loves a good panda, and ours is no exception. He's the perfect mix of business and fun, the definition of cool. He's charming, fluffy, a perfect gentleman, and an unbelievable

PANDA PREMIERE

DudePerfect.com

MASCOTS

Tyler's first mascot idea was a fainting goat. If you don't know what one of those looks like, you're about to find out.

youtube.com/watch?v=we9_CdNPuJg

MEET THE DUDES

Panda

Go Big Moment: Hang gliding over an active volcano in '08

Go Big Dream: To meet YouTube's famous sneezing panda

My Best Kept Secret: Currently dating Hayden Pandattiere

Favorite Shot: My sick dunk in Sacramento

DudePerfect.com

dancer. He is better than we are at everything. He was born, or in this case made, in China. We call him "Panda."

At first, the idea was small: get a cool Panda costume and make funny videos. But then we tried on the suit, and it freaking rocked. Very quickly, Panda became more to us than just a costume. Panda became a member of our team.

No doubt, Panda has been one of the most fun parts of Dude Perfect. After we introduced him to our audience, we started bringing him into public with us. The best place for this was at Texas A&M basketball games. We never could have anticipated how much people would love hanging out with Panda in real life. At first we got to games early in order to sit where the camera would see Panda. We quickly learned that this was unnecessary. Because the fans love him, Panda sits wherever he wants, whenever he wants. He's fun to be around and attracts plenty of attention, making him a camera magnet. People know that if they sit by him, they'll end up on the big screen, which is kind of a big deal.

But no one likes the camera—and the attention—more than Panda. And although I can think of countless stories to illustrate this, one moment stands high above the rest. Let me set the stage.

It's moments after a Texas A&M basketball game, one of the most important of the season. It's ESPN's rivalry week, and because of the importance of the game and the hype surrounding it, coach Bobby Knight and legendary announcer Brent Musburger are on-site to cover the game. After the final buzzer sounds, the guys and I turn to leave, ready to beat the crowd to the door. But we're missing two members of our crew: Coby and Panda. Coby is sometimes hard to find, but Panda, not so much. We spot the large, walking Oreo on the opposite side of the arena, down in the first row. From that far away, it's tough to tell what's going on. Once we figure it out, though, it makes perfect sense. Knight and Musburger are hosting ESPN's post-game commentary, and Panda—unsurprisingly—has bolted straight for the camera. He not only waves to the country but, by watching himself in the monitor, makes it look like he pats Bobby Knight's head. Nice.

Until now, people have seen Panda and know what he's about, but what they haven't learned is what it's like to *be* Panda. We knew from the beginning that we'd take turns wearing the Panda suit, and at first, I was nervous that Panda would be really different depending on who was rockin' the costume. But I was wrong. When you put on the Panda suit, or "Panda up," as we call it, Panda doesn't become you—you become Panda. Wearing the suit changes you, and for whatever reason, anyone wearing the suit takes on the same personality. The suit makes you feel invincible because everything you do looks either cool or hilarious. You get away with dance moves you'd never attempt without the suit. If you want to spread your arms out and spin around, just do it—you're Panda.

Panda has zero self-confidence issues. He is friendly, enter-taining, and always the center of attention. But most important, Panda has the ability to make people feel special. When he opens the door for people, waves at them, or gives a hug, he's not just doing something nice; he's bringing joy. From inside the suit, it's fun to see the sparkle in a little girl's eye when you bend down to give her a bear hug. To her, I guess it's the same type of feeling as being hugged by Mickey Mouse at Disney World. It's exciting, and she feels like Panda is her friend. Since doing these simple, everyday things makes people so happy, it makes sense for whoever is in the Panda suit to assume the role of the friendly, enthusiastic Panda.

The main drawback to the suit is that it's almost impossible to see out of. The suit's eyes are each about the size of a straw, so you can barely see anything. Enter the "Panda spotter," Panda's right-hand man. It took us about four seconds to realize how important this job was for Panda's success—and safety. Poles, trays of food, high fives, cars—these things come out of nowhere, so what Panda can't see coming, the Panda spotter has to. The spotter's main responsibilities include keeping Panda safe, making sure he high-fives stray hands in the aisles, and getting Panda into all the pictures he's asked to be in.

The spotter is also responsible for talking for Panda. The spotter traditionally says things like, "Over here, Panda! Watch out for that girl! Sorry, you'll have to excuse Panda; he's kind of blind." It's a funny sight: a college guy holding a panda's hand, guiding him to where he needs to go.

And it almost never fails. As the spotter does his thing, someone asks, "Wait, why can't the Panda talk?"

We generally smile and respond, "Good question, but have you ever seen a panda talk? Me neither. Get serious."

Now that you've imagined what it's like to "Panda up," I want you to imagine you're a college basketball player in your prime. You're playing against well-ranked Texas A&M, amidst their almost deafening crowd. The game, hanging in the balance, depends on the free throws you're about to take. As you step up to the line, you take a deep breath and focus—you've trained for this situation. You skillfully zone out the noise of the crowd, and for a moment, everything goes quiet, even the thoughts in your head. You're lifting your arms to shoot, but your eyes, focused as they are, alert you to something moving in the stands. It's not a well-painted sign. It's not a cheerleader. It's a Panda. And it's jumping down the stairs. *What?* You try to think about something else—anything else. Reality checks back in. You're still holding the basketball. You're almost out of time. You can't wait any longer. Your vision is blurry, but you shoot because you have to, and through the haze you see the vague shape of a ball clank hard off the rim. A&M gets the rebound. Panda raises his arms in triumph. The crowd goes crazy.

Like it or not, Panda will always be the center of attention, no matter who you are or what you try to focus on. And that, more than anything else, is why we love him. In reality, it's just a costume, but as our mascot, as a member of our team, Panda has an uncanny ability to turn people's attention from what they're doing toward what *he's* doing. And what's the most common response when people watch our Panda dance, high-five, open a door, throw a basketball, or leap distractingly down the stairs? They smile—uncontrollably—and they laugh. Our Panda, a simple costume, unites an entire crowd simply by unifying their emotions.

This chapter begins a new section, one in which we'll examine the second-to-last Go Big principle. So far in your Go Big journey, we've talked about the Get Excited passion you need to launch your vision, the Own It mentality you need to pursue it, and the Blink Later mind-set you need to have in order to capitalize on opportunities. The next principle is one that will help you tackle one of the biggest buzzwords in the connected world—*momentum.*

We know there are many different ways to create and sustain

TRICK SHOOTING 101

If your panda tries to make a flaming basketball shot, make sure you have a fire extinguisher on hand. Panda fur is very flammable.

momentum, but we're convinced one strategy towers above the rest. From everything we've experienced, lasting momentum always begins with inspiration. That's why the fourth Go Big principle is Inspire Others.

Momentum—as far as an organization is concerned—is the unified movement of a group of people in a certain direction. Momentum is all about having people behind you and beside you, taking unified action toward a common goal. We believe this happens best when people rally around a common idea, person, cause, or feeling.

We saw this happen with Panda. The first time we took Panda to an A&M basketball game, people laughed, took pictures with him, and generally thought he was awesome. On his second trip, a few groups remembered him and called out, "Panda! Panda!" from all across the student section. Word was getting around.

The third time Panda made an appearance, some serious momentum had formed. About ten minutes before the game, Panda entered the arena from an upstairs doorway and made his way down toward the first couple of rows. He didn't get very far. As soon as the students realized he had entered the building, voices yelled out, "The Panda's here! Hey, there's the Panda! Look, over there!" Before we knew it, around five thousand people rose to their feet, a bass-thumping "Panda! Panda! Panda! . . ." chant formed, and something rose above the students' heads. Round pieces of paper glued to paint stirring sticks bounced up and down in our direction. One piece held still long enough

Momentum— as far as an organization is concerned— is the unified movement of a group of people in a certain direction.

for us to tell what it was. Printed on every one of those pieces of paper was the face of a panda. We waded through the pressing crowd and saw what turned out to be the icing on the cake. Facing the court and the cameras, students raised huge black-and-white signs that said, "Pandamonium!"

There was more happening in that arena than cheers, panda faces, and "Pandamonium" signs. The Texas A&M fans had rallied behind our Dude Perfect Panda. And as that arena came unglued, you could see, hear, and feel the momentum.

This idea isn't limited to just our story either. Recently, a guy in Massachusetts tweeted to the mayor of Detroit that a statue of RoboCop (the title character from a 1987 movie about a half-man, half-machine police officer who protects the streets of Detroit) should be built somewhere inside city limits. The mayor's discouraging response quickly launched an online frenzy of discussion over the necessity of a RoboCop statue. Only weeks later, by combining Facebook, Twitter, and a fund-raising website called Kickstarter.com, people near and far had teamed up to fund and build a life-size statue of RoboCop on the grounds of Detroit's Roosevelt Park. DetroitNeedsRoboCop.com, the landing page for the campaign, has united givers around the slogan "Serve the public trust, protect the innocent, uphold the awesome." In the spirit of a better, safer Detroit, givers from all over the world have amassed more than $65,000, plenty to accomplish the task.

A simple idea can rally people together in incredible ways. And in this case, one of the coolest parts about the story is that out of the community established around this comical idea, a group called RoboCharity has been formed, one that will use

GO BIG TIP

One of the best ways to gain and sustain lasting momentum is to inspire others.

the group's already assembled momentum to help the city in ways a statue might not be able to.

Whether you already have a significant amount of momentum behind your Go Big dream or not, one of the best ways to gain and sustain lasting momentum is to inspire others. Over the next couple of chapters, we'll get into more specifics about different ways to inspire others, those outside as well as those inside your team. But for starters, we want to suggest one way to inspire your audience: give them something to rally around. An iconic figure (unfortunately, Panda is taken), a contest, a charity, a theme song, an event, even a secret handshake—it doesn't have to be fancy or expensive. It just needs to be something likable, something that people will *want* to identify with, something that will form your audience into a momentum-filled group—a group pointed in your brand's direction.

The key to eventually capitalizing on this momentum is to choose something that—once people identify with and rally around it—will allow your audience to further connect with your brand. For us, one of our highest priorities has always been to brand Dude Perfect as *fun*. So when we chose a mascot, we wanted something that mirrored that idea. We could have chosen any mascot—a powerful lion, a terrifying dragon, a creepy gargoyle. Instead, we chose a fun, fluffy, likable Panda. We wanted something that felt like us. When people rally around Panda, they rally around Dude Perfect. And this Panda-momentum is almost out of control. Whenever we go through a stretch of Panda-free videos, many of our online viewers cry out for more Panda. To say the least, Panda has left quite an impression.

A lot of people assume that as Dude Perfect grows, surely we will ditch Panda. They think that since he doesn't have anything to do with basketball, we'll move on to some other mascot or leave him behind. Dude Perfect *is* a little different than it was when we first started, but we're still the same guys, and we're still about fun. That's why we still use Panda. Panda is an incredible way for us to show the world that we don't take ourselves too seriously. It's an awesome way for us to keep an element of fun in the public eye—something any smart brand should do. People like fun, and they gravitate toward groups that have it.

And hey, we can't forget the most important reason Panda's still around: Texas A&M basketball. All we can say is . . . clear the stairs.

CHAPTER 15
TROLLS

Texas A&M has a cool old saying: "From the outside looking in, you can't understand it. From the inside looking out, you can't explain it." Being Aggies ourselves, the Dude Perfect crew would admit there's something special about belonging to the Texas A&M family. We would also admit that, as the saying suggests, it's difficult to put into words exactly why we love A&M so much. But believe it or not, the reason we can't explain it *isn't* that we spent too much time riding cows to school. The problem isn't our ability to explain it; it's other people's ability to relate to it.

When you're on the inside of something truly special, something that affects you down to your core, something with purpose, fun, meaning, passion, tradition, competition, excellence, and inspiration all intertwined, you can tell all the stories you want, but if the other people haven't also experienced those moments, they can never really understand the look in your eye when you talk about it. In their minds, you sound crazy. But in yours, they missed out on more than they'll ever know.

You and I both know this concept applies to more than just the appeal of hallowed Texas A&M University. I believe this idea appears clearly in the lives of all Go Big dreamers. If you've been chasing a dream for a while now, you might already know where I'm heading with this; in fact, you're probably nodding your head in agreement. On the other hand, if you're just launching your Go Big journey, you'll be discovering this truth very soon.

Here it is: those sitting on the sidelines of your unique vision, your team, and your passion-driven pursuit of the dream you were designed to chase—those people can never fully understand what you're so relentlessly chasing. The reason is simple. It's not their dream. And because they haven't been in this particular process with you, they can't possibly understand it. They can't relate to the passions that led you to your dream in the first place. They can't relate to the sleep you lose as idea after idea races through your mind. They can't go back in time and experience the countless hours that have led up to your current position. So what do they do? How do they handle this inability to relate? Some of them choose to hate. They hate on you, they hate on your team, they hate on the time you spend and the way you spend it. They take their lack of understanding and vastly underestimate the worth of your dream. Ladies and gentlemen, I would like to introduce you to the haters, or as they're called in the Internet world, the trolls.

This section is all about the fourth Go Big principle, Inspire Others. In short, we have found that by inspiring others, you can create lasting momentum for your organization. And because that is one of the greatest ways to gain momentum, it's important to explain how you can guard that momentum from the haters—the trolls—who are out to destroy it.

In our YouTube world, this is how it works. The Dude Perfect crew comes up with a fresh idea that will help us continue to pursue our dream—a cool new video, for example. As soon as we release this video, as soon as it goes live, we start getting feedback from viewers. The first batch of comments is usually positive. The people who get to the new content first are generally some of our more closely connected viewers, and since they have a better understanding of who we are as a group, they tend to enjoy and appreciate the video. As time passes, however, the trolls get wind of the new video, and with it a fresh opportunity for them to wreak havoc. Now a troll—to give you a better understanding of the term—is anyone who purposefully stirs up arguments on online message boards, blogs, and in this case, YouTube comment pages. Their comments are often extreme—because they're intended to be. A troll's comments are designed to get an emotional reaction from others.

For just a moment, the guys and I would like to applaud the trolls. We believe in giving credit where credit is due, and without a doubt, credit is due here. Most trolls are great at what they do. They are professional argument starters. Trolls know that everyone has an argument button, and they know how to push it. With one simple comment, a troll can create a lengthy conversation revolving around his statement. Trolls can get nice people, well-behaved children, and role-model parents to come unglued. They can get an entire group of people, often hundreds and hundreds of viewers, to temporarily shift their focus toward them. To the troll, it's a game, and like a casino, the house always wins. If a troll can engage someone in a hostile conversation long enough, eventually the other person will snap. I've seen it more times than I can count.

Now I'll admit that while these conversations get out of hand nine out of ten times, they can sometimes be hilarious. Watching people lose their cool is entertaining, and we find ourselves reading these comments, waiting for the fuse to light, burn, and explode in language more colorful than any Fourth of July fireworks I've seen. The explosions are why trolls mess with people in the first place. A troll is the online version of an older brother teasing his little sister simply to get a reaction.

But funny or not, a troll can affect more than just the other viewers. If you and I aren't careful, a troll—or any hater, for that matter—can affect us. In fact, if we don't handle the criticism quickly and correctly, our momentum will suffer. For example, when we released our first video surrounding the GMC campaign, a group of people instantly complained that we were "selling out," insisting that they liked us better before we linked Dude Perfect with another company. I'll be honest—that was hard to hear. We'd poured our efforts into something new, and we wanted our supporters to back us a hundred percent. Unfortunately, that's not what happened. One of the parts that hurt the most was that even though most of the negative comments belonged to trolls, a couple of them didn't. We noticed that some of the viewers who'd had nothing but positive things to say in the past were clearly against this new idea, an idea we cared a lot about.

So what did we do, and what should you do when you encounter criticism from the outside? First of all, remind yourself that risk is a natural part of every Go Big dream . . . and

TROLL COMMENTS

Commenting about the Kyle Field Shot, one troll said, "You can tell it's fake because you can see the ball curve, and wind couldn't do that. I did the calculations with a standard-weight ball, and you would need a hurricane to make it move like that. Not even a knuckleball moves that much."

take a deep breath. Then, consider the incoming voices and ask yourself, *Whose opinion really matters here? Who holds sway over your life?* Is it the troll? Is it some random person on Facebook? Is it your family? Is it your team? Is it your audience? If good advice from wise people led you into this now-controversial decision, are you going to throw aside that advice as soon as you run into resistance from the public?

We didn't. Looking at the feedback from our GMC videos, there were viewers in both camps. Some were thrilled we were expanding our Dude Perfect horizons, and some were hoping we'd stay as we'd always been and leave other companies out of the equation. But instead of basing our decision about future company involvement strictly on our viewers, we focused on the opinions of people with a big-picture view of what was really happening: a couple of guys working corporately for YouTube, some businessmen who had advised us in the past, and Mr. T, our fearless business manager. We realized that although a few of our loyal viewers were nervous about the decision, those viewers didn't really have the big-picture understanding of the plan that we did.

So we chose to move forward with company involvement in the future, at least every once in a while. If we had listened to the few dissatisfied people instead of the opinions we knew were most relevant to the decision, we would have walked away from some of the coolest opportunities we've had to date, including some of the viewers' favorites. That said, it would have been foolish not to listen to any of the criticism. What we've learned is that while you don't usually need to take *extreme* criticism to heart, if you dial down those extreme comments a few notches, you'll usually come up with helpful feedback. When a couple

GO BIG TIP

Risk is a natural part of every Go Big dream.

of trolls said it was the end of the world for Dude Perfect to work with corporate sponsors, it was easy to see how extreme that statement was. On the other hand, viewed through a less extreme lens, we could see how problems *would* arise if we only did company-based stuff instead of the raw videos people were used to seeing from us. Because of this discussion, we decided to aim for a balance between the two, and it has worked really well so far.

Hearing voices all around you and being able to zone out the ones that don't matter—that's hard. Our human tendency is to react and, like some of our viewers on the Internet, snap at the attacks of the trolls in our lives. It takes a certain skill to keep the negative voices around you from getting inside your head. It's like a heated game of basketball. The best players know how to get inside the opposing players' heads, how to take them out of the game by frustrating them to the point where they lose all focus. On the other hand, those same players know how to ignore the other team's attempts to throw them off their game; instead, they stay focused on the plan they know is crucial to their team's success. The key for those athletes—and for you and me—is one of our favorite things in the whole world, something the guys and I believe is one of the greatest characteristics a human being can develop: *mental toughness.*

Mental toughness says to haters and competitors alike, "You can say or do whatever you want, but I'm not fazed." Tyler in particular claims to be one of the most mentally tough people on the planet. He claims to have mentally overcome mono in one day. Diagnosed in the morning, he went home and said, "Not happening; this is football season. I don't have time for this." He got checked again the next day—no mono. I wasn't

GO BIG TIP

While you don't usually need to take *extreme* criticism to heart, if you dial down those extreme comments a few notches, you'll usually come up with helpful feedback.

there during Ty's high school days, so I can neither confirm nor deny this ridiculous story, but what I do know is that Ty, the guy who made a shot out of an airplane in two tries, is mentally tough. It's mental toughness that ultimately allows you to hear the haters but not *listen* to them. It's mental toughness that helps you focus on the advice of the wise people around you. It's mental toughness that, apparently, helps you overcome mono.

Finally, since the negativity will be constant, another common temptation is to pursue your goals in order to prove those people wrong. And while using other people's doubts to fuel your fire isn't all bad, it's important to remember that the real reason you're pursuing your dream is far bigger than proving some troll wrong. If you can keep your focus on the real reason behind your passions, you'll be far more effective in your pursuits than if you're simply trying to stick it to some hater. Keep your thoughts on the bigger purpose of your dream, and stay focused on the reasons you were excited about pursuing it in the first place.

THE TIM TEBOW COMMERCIAL

youtube.com/watch?v=WO8imsZl1F8

That said, every once in a while, it's nice to look back and see how you were able to rise above the doubts and negativity that surrounded you. Tim Tebow—Heisman-winning quarterback of the Florida Gators and current NFL star—is a prime example. In a commercial aired around the last Super Bowl, Tebow listed off the things that others said he *couldn't* do, things that, of course, he *did* do. Tebow didn't focus his efforts on proving haters wrong. If he had, he probably wouldn't be where he is today. But he did allow the doubts and negativity of others to make him stronger. He allowed the haters' comments to fuel his desire to improve, to pursue excellence, and to achieve his dream of becoming an NFL quarterback. Now he is able to look in the camera and say with conviction, "They said I couldn't . . . I appreciate that."

Tebow. Basketball. Mental toughness. It all points to the same principle: When you're pursuing your Go Big dream, you can't afford to get bogged down by the negativity of others. Since those outside your team will usually underestimate your dream's worth, you have to realize that the best thing to do is decide whose opinions matter the most and base your decisions on those voices.

Keep your focus on your dream. Listen to the opinions that matter; zone out the rest. It's why racehorses wear blinders over their eyes. By shielding out the action to the left and right of the horses' view, jockeys are able to keep their horses completely focused on the front-facing path. If we are going to chase our Go Big dreams, we have to focus on what we know we have to do and not get distracted by others. Our momentum and the future of our Go Big visions are at stake.

GO BIG TIP

Keep your focus on your dream. Listen to the opinions that matter; zone out the rest.

CHAPTER 16

COOL THINGS

This chapter will feel out of place. It will feel tossed in and random. And that's exactly the point. Your life, as well as ours, is kind of like this book. For the most part, each chapter works about the same way. And that's great because even if you're an anti-schedule person like me, you need a certain amount of structure to keep your mind from going crazy. However, if we're not careful, our lives, and even the pursuit of our Go Big dreams, can drift into a routine that, before we know it, sucks the inspiration right out of us.

Now, if you've been paying attention to this section, you know how key your ability to inspire others is to your Go Big dream. You know that losing this ability would be a serious problem. Fortunately, there's a solution.

Up until now, anytime I've identified a problem, I've simply explained what we in Dude Perfect believe is the solution. But now I think it's time to do something different. In this chapter, I'm going to let you *experience* the solution. Confused? Awesome. Let's start.

The guys and I have some sophisticated wisdom that we would like to pass on. And by that I mean we have learned some cool things that may or may not have any direct bearing on your dream, but will be fun to experience. The three things I'm going to tell you about may not change your life, but they will change your perspective. And they just might help you retain your excitement as you pursue your Go Big dream.

✦ ✦ ✦

About a year ago, I was eating at the McAlister's Deli in College Station with some friends. Drew, a good friend, said to me, "Cory, you know that putting Splenda on a lemon makes it taste exactly like an orange, right?"

You're probably thinking something frighteningly similar to what I told Drew: "Okay, all kidding aside, this conversation is over."

But it wasn't over; he wouldn't let it go. He insisted he wasn't messing with me, but he couldn't stop smiling while he said it. He tried to act like it was common knowledge, which of course, being a made-up thing, it wasn't.

When he kept going on about it, I got curious, which is exactly what he wanted. Everyone else at the table was on my side, and none of us could tell if he was joking. His lousy poker face was making me mad, but if what he said was true, that would be a fantastic secret. At this point, I just had to know. I called over our super nice waitress, apologized for what was

TRICK SHOOTING 101

If you're in downtown New York and need to use the bathroom, the Trump Tower is open to the public, and the bathrooms are sweet!

about to be a complete waste of her time, explained the situation, and asked for a few lemon slices we could use to make our lemon-Splenda combos. She brought some back, saying we'd made her curious and she'd come back later to hear the result.

Drew prepared a lemon slice by taking a pack of Splenda and sprinkling both sides with pixie dust. Seeing it on the plate made me want to take back my promise to play Drew's game. It looked dumb: a lemon with fake sugar on it.

He slid the plate toward me, and instantly my chance to bail was gone. Laughing at Drew for asking me to do this and laughing at myself for agreeing, I picked up the snow-covered lemon. Raising it to my mouth, I made a final bet in my mind. No way.

I closed my eyes and slowly bit into the juicy lemon slice. As I did, my mind talked to me in a distinctly orange voice.

I thought you said this was a lemon.

Cory, this is an orange.

Cory, you're eating an orange.

I can't explain it, and I don't even want to try. It didn't *kind of* taste like an orange; it tasted like the *best* orange I'd ever had. It tasted like one of the oranges you see in the commercials where a smiling man climbs a ladder and reaches for a tree-hanging orange covered in sunlight. Someone had picked that orange and put it in my hand.

I'm not trying to be dramatic. If I hadn't known I was holding a lemon and hadn't spent the last thirty minutes talking about it, I would have confidently told you that the fruit I'd blindly eaten was an incredibly delicious orange.

I didn't have to tell the others what I thought; they could see it in my eyes. The skepticism was gone; confused delight had washed over me. For a moment, my whole world turned orange. Thoughts flooded in. *This is unbelievable. The perfect first-date icebreaker. I could bet people anything. How does no one know about this? Does Splenda even know? I should buy stock. Lemons and Splenda are free at restaurants—how much longer can that last? Another month, tops.*

I snapped back to reality when our waitress walked up to our table. She smiled and asked me if it was true, and since I couldn't stop smiling when I told her yes, she was probably as skeptical as ever, but I can promise you she tried it later that night. If she's reading this, I know she's a free orange fan.

I still don't understand how, but it works and it's awesome. Also, we don't know why, but it only works with Splenda. So make sure you use Splenda when you test this for yourself. We know this secret will spread fast, and that's good. We want people to enjoy free oranges for as long as they can. But we also know this won't last forever. All too quickly, restaurants' free lemon and Splenda supplies that we're all so used to seeing will become too sought after to remain free. The best way to prevent this is to go to SaveFreeOranges.com and help us fight the inevitable.

Seriously, go there. We bought that website.

JOIN THE RESISTANCE

We need your help to save free oranges! Visit our website and keep free oranges free.

savefreeoranges.com

✦ ✦ ✦

Like it or not, we just changed your perception of restaurant life. Now we're going to do the same thing with your driving life. Get excited.

We've all been there. You're driving down the road on a sunny day, just minding your own business, when all of a sudden, you pass a car wearing a decal from your rival college or professional sports team.

You roll your eyes as quickly as possible, but it's too late. That hideous logo is stuck in your mind. Unwilling to accept this small defeat, you desperately want to do something about it. You wish there was a way to really stick it to them. Turns out, there is. Dude Perfect would like to introduce you to "Windshield Wipering."

The concept is simple. You calmly get in front of someone and stay five or six car lengths ahead of him. Then, whenever you're ready, you turn on your windshield wiper fluid and hold it in the "on" position. What you'll notice is that, if you're going over thirtyish miles per hour, your car will spray a mist over your windshield and, yes, behind you toward the unsuspecting but deserving rival sports team fan.

Then, as you casually glance in your rearview mirror, you see the fish take the bait. Confused as to why it's raining on such a clear sunny day, the understandably unintelligent rival sports fan turns on his windshield wipers, trying to fight off the tiny rain cloud he assumes must be hovering above his car. Here's the best part. The rest of the world thinks you're simply cleaning your windshield—and cleaning it well—but you know the truth. So as much fun as it would be to keep your little prank a secret, you'd rather the person behind you know that you and your sports team owns his.

So as soon as you and/or any other passengers with you see the trailing car take the bait, have everyone in your vehicle throw up their hands in victorious celebration. Unless you drive a car with tinted windows, the loser behind you will see your celebration, connect the dots, and notice his rival team's logo

TRICK SHOOTING 101

A great time to windshield wiper someone is right before it rains. They're already prepared to turn on their wipers; you're just giving them a reason to do it sooner.

on your car. Like I said, this is a simple idea, but its results are incredibly fulfilling.

Try it on your own rival sports fan, roommate, or mom.

✦   ✦   ✦

Ty and I are basically like Jason Bourne—we notice everything— so we keep a running list of interesting stuff. Our favorite list is one that Ty started: The World's Biggest Misconceptions. One day as we were driving to the ranch, Ty enlightened us with his list of things that sound good, but just don't make any sense:

"To start off—*There's no such thing as a dumb question.* Wow. No one believes that. I have heard plenty of dumb questions everywhere, all the time.

"*It's the thought that counts.* Yeah? Try this: it's your mom's birthday. 'Mom, I really thought about getting you a present, but I just didn't.' That's not gonna work. You'll be in trouble— with your dad, most likely. It's not the thought that counts, and whoever tells you that just doesn't want to get you a present.

"*There's a first time for everything.* Again, I don't know how this stuff gets started. I will probably never be stepped on by an elephant.

"*Practice makes perfect.* When was the last time you met someone perfect at something? *Never* is the answer—ever. You never have. Well, except Jesus—but that's different.

"*It's not about winning or losing; it's about having fun.* Ha— please. That's what I would say too . . . if I lost all the time.

"*You can do anything you put your mind to.* No, you can't. I could not just be like, 'I wanna have lasers shoot out of my

TRICK SHOOTING 101

If you pick up a phone in the hallway of a nice hotel and say, "Blue Bell ice cream, ninth floor," there's a good possibility Blue Bell ice cream will appear on the ninth floor.

eyes and cut down that tree.' That doesn't work. I can't put my whole mind into that and make it happen. Misconception—that's why it's on the list!"

+ + +

First of all, I realize this is a lot to wrap your mind around. When we were doing these things I mentioned, we didn't have to take the time to think about how good they were for us. We didn't think about how the lemon-orange broke a mold for our minds—letting us see the world in a different, bigger way. We didn't celebrate that windshield wipering turned a boring task—driving—into a fun and victorious one. And we didn't discuss or consciously memo ourselves that the "misconceptions" list flips the world on its head, exercising our brains to reexamine what we've been told our whole lives. We didn't think about these results at the time. We were just having fun—but the results still happened.

Your brain—full of excitement, creativity, and inspiration—is like a sponge. But keep focused on just one thing long enough, even a Go Big thing, and eventually that brain of yours will dry up. Now, as Go Big dreamers, you and I both know how important it is to keep that from happening.

So what do we do? We fight routine with random. We fight the stagnating, drying effects of the everyday by giving our minds an outlet, a way to breathe deeply and soak back in the cool, vibrant, invigorating energy that can begin to disappear. That may sound hard to do, but in reality it's not.

The trick is to have fun. Have fun thinking about and doing

COOL THINGS FORMULA

Here's our professional formula. Cool Things: Think about them. Do them. Feel better.

spontaneous, awesome things that interest and excite you. This doesn't mean doing stupid, illegal stuff so you can get a rush of adrenaline. It means eating free oranges, windshield wipering a rival sports fan behind you, and laughing about misconceptions. It means playing real basketball, swimming, playing your guitar, going fishing. It means having fun. Why? Because *fun is refreshing*.

Here's the deal. If we said we didn't care about fun, you wouldn't believe us. If you've ever seen one of our videos, the fun factor in Dude Perfect is pretty clear. Because of that, we're not ashamed to say that we believe one of your highest priorities, both as an organization and as an individual, should be to have fun. We believe an element of fun is key to any successful business. We believe that most people take themselves way too seriously, and most companies only do things that have an official cause and effect related to the bottom line. We believe they're missing out.

Since this section of the book is about inspiring others, what we want to convey with this chapter is that doing cool things, exercising your creativity and fun muscle, is key to remaining relevant, likable, sane, energized, and excited about your dream. So, use the examples we listed earlier or come up with your own, and make sure you're consistently doing fun things. It will keep your mind—and in turn your dream—fresh.

Finally, and this is incredibly important, do things that expand your creativity.

In our opinion, Google is a company that seems to fully understand the weight of this concept. In order to spark and maintain an atmosphere of extreme creativity, Google allows its employees what they call "20 percent time." Four days out

GO BIG TIP

Exercising your creativity and fun muscle is key to remaining relevant, likable, sane, energized, and excited about your dream. Remember: *Fun is refreshing.*

of the week, Google employees do what most other employees do—assignments. But on their fifth day, their 20 percent time, Google employees are given the freedom to work on company-related projects that are of personal interest to them. By allowing this practice, already passionate employees are given the opportunity to pursue projects that feel most exciting to them. In the midst of their work, they are encouraged to pursue projects that are fun.

I think 20 percent time has got to be one of the greatest ideas in corporate history. By giving its employees a certain amount of do-whatever-you-want time, Google allows the employees' minds to expand well beyond their job descriptions. Google, in essence, unlocks the creative potential of its team members.

Google has found this free-form, laid-back atmosphere to be an effective way for its engineers to refresh and stimulate their all-important brains. And because each employee is working on something personally exciting, the results are phenomenal. In fact, in an article about Google's 20 percent time, the *New York Times* echoes one of the truths we've been exploring since the beginning of this book—that your excitement is key to your potential for excellence. The article's author, a Google engineer himself, writes, "People work better when they're involved in something they're passionate about."

So this program and the concept of exercising your creativity really worth the hype? Just how good are the ideas that come out of 20 percent time?

Well, you decide. Do you think *Gmail* was a good idea?

Take it from Google, and take it from me: do things that expand your creativity. My suggestion is to create your own "20 percent time," to always have some type of side project going on, something that truly interests you. Write a book. Play a song. Design your dream home. Paint a mural. Build a model airplane. Maybe even create a life-size statue of RoboCop. Do something that will positively stretch your creativity. It will be fun, and it will be time well spent.

CHAPTER 17
YOU MIGHT BE A TRICK SHOOTER IF . . .

As you look over your shoulder, you see the basketball goal out of the corner of your eye. You move a couple of steps to the right, and yeah, that's perfect; now you're directly lined up. You look back over your shoulder once more, face the opposite way, and throw the ball over your head toward the goal.

Maybe you turn around to see if it went in. Maybe, staring straight ahead, you play the *Please, I'm so confident I don't even have to look* card. Most of the time, you miss. But every once in a while . . . *swish.* Shooting blind is exhilarating—and hearing the eventual excitement behind you makes it all worthwhile. It's a classic trick shot, and if you've spent much time attempting trick shots of your own, you've probably tried it. I know I have.

Maybe the backward shot isn't your style. Maybe you rock the bounce shot, the long shot, or every mom's favorite, the increasingly popular rooftop roller. Whatever trick shot is your favorite to shoot, you know that every time you see a video of

TRICK SHOOTING 101

When attempting a field goal shot, make sure your snapper/center avoids standing up right in the middle of the kick.

161

someone else's that looks similar to yours, you instantly understand what it took to make that shot. If you're shooting backward, you know how hard it is to make the adjustment when you can't even see where your ball went. If it's the long shot, you know that the wind can catch it and make your tenth try look way worse than your first. You've been there, so you feel for the person hitting a shot similar to yours.

There is an invisible bond between trick basketball shooters. If you've never tried it, you might think I'm crazy; if you have, you've been tracking with these last couple of paragraphs and know exactly what I'm talking about. You know what it's like to laugh at a friend who just can't seem to tackle a certain shot, and until you actually try, you're almost positive you could make it the very first time. You've probably said, or at least heard someone say, "Trust me—that's a lot harder than it looks." You're a student by day and a trick shooter by night, or by weekend, or whenever the car's not parked under the hoop.

If you've ever filmed a trick shot, you know your hand gets tired waiting for the person shooting to nail it. You know that no matter how many times you tell the shooter to shoot it harder, he or she is probably going to keep shooting it exactly the same way, hoping for a different result. But of course, when it's your turn to shoot, you also forget to listen to the person holding the camera, the person with the best view, and you do it the way *you* think it needs to be done.

And finally, if you're a trick shooter, you know that whether it's you or one of your friends, when that really cool shot finally goes in, that shot you've been working on for what seems like forever, you go crazy and yell and run somewhere, anywhere, and high-five and chest-bump and rush over to the camera to see how it looked. And you laugh and know that all the waiting, rebounding, encouraging, and filming was definitely worth it. Because you're a trick shooter—yes, because *you* are a trick shooter—you know that there are no regrets after an awesome make.

Now if you or I had read this two years ago, I'd be surprised if we would have felt what we feel now, if we would have understood the experience of making a cool trick shot. That's because over the last two years, the online trick shooting community has really taken off.

We're not sure how much of that is due to Dude Perfect; surely some of it is. So if you started because you saw us do it and thought it looked fun, we're honored to be an inspiration for you. But whether you started in order to imitate somebody else or, like us, just stumbled into it while competing against friends, you're here, and we're all better for it.

The proof that this community has grown is undeniable. It's all over YouTube. The night we posted our very first video, we searched for "trick basketball shots" and "amazing basketball shots" on YouTube, and only a handful of videos came up. Of those videos, most had to do with either college or professional basketball. Of the ones that didn't, the ones we would all consider true trick basketball videos, only three or four had more than a hundred views. Only three or four—that's basically nothing. Just now I ran the same search—"amazing basketball shots"—and there are over 10,000 listed! Now check this out. If you were to Google "trick basketball shots," our website—DudePerfect.com—would come up on the first page, along with a staggering 13,000,000 other results. That's absolutely unreal! Think about it. On April 8, 2009, we posted our very

TRICK SHOOTING 101

If attempting a water-balloon launcher shot from the back of a pickup truck, make sure you aim well above the truck bed's light.

first video. In a little over two years, the change has been absolutely incredible. We know it's not all due to us, but we hope we've had a big hand in it. Trick shots are fun, and if we've been able to help others enjoy this passion with us, we're honored.

Every single day, we get e-mails and YouTube messages from fellow trick shooters. They suggest shots for us to try next. They ask us to watch their videos, give them advice, and to be friends with them on Facebook. Maybe you could have guessed all that. Maybe you've even written in or sent us a video yourself. For a moment, let's pretend you did. What you might not know is that we do watch an incredible number of your videos and read a ton of your messages. We wish there were a better way to talk with everyone who writes in or sends us their videos, to tell them how great their shots are and how much we appreciate their encouragement. I try to write back as much as I can, but even when I don't get a chance to, I can tell you there's something really cool about getting a message or seeing a video from someone inspired by something we've done. Every single time, *every single time*, it puts a smile on my face. So don't stop suggesting shots and don't stop sending us your best stuff, because out of everything we get to do, this might just be our favorite part.

If you're not a trick shooter, you might be wondering why we'd spend a whole chapter talking about this newborn trick shot community. Well, besides the fact that these hardworking guys and girls deserve a serious shout-out, this growing community of trick shot enthusiasts is an incredible example of what every smart entrepreneur and Go Big dreamer should be aiming for: *momentum*. We've been talking about this concept for a few chapters now, and in the last few pages of the Inspire Others section, we want to make one final thought clear.

If one of your organization's main goals is momentum—and it should be—your time and energy will be better spent inspiring others than simply trying to persuade them. Take the five-year-old version of me, for example. For almost that whole year, I carried this cool little blanket with me everywhere—I called it "bop-bee," no idea why. To me, that blanket was the greatest thing ever. The two of us were inseparable. But one day, sitting in a movie theater with Coby and the rest of my family, I sailed all the way to Never Never Land in a magical, pixie-dusted Peter Pan boat. And during the sixty-minute voyage, the weirdest thing happened. My grip on bop-bee got weaker and weaker. Finally, as the movie ended and credits rolled, I stood up and thrust the blanket into my mom's hands. I knew there could only be one Peter Pan, but the way I saw it, there was plenty of room for another Lost Boy. That day, when I walked out of *Peter Pan* for the first time, I didn't kind of want to be a Lost Boy; I thought I *was* a Lost Boy. So with bop-bee out of the picture, what did I carry around instead? Only the greatest Lost Boy knife Toys"R"Us had to offer. And who did I fight? Classic dumb question. Coby, obviously. And I won every time.

If you had tried to persuade me to give up bop-bee, you would have been wasting your time. Sure, you might have been able to trade me an ice cream sandwich for five minutes away from my blanket, but the moment I was finished eating, bop-bee was back. Persuasion, whether a convincing argument or an enticing treat, is external motivation, and it can only last so long. Peter and the Lost Boys, on the other hand, didn't persuade me of anything; they *inspired* me. That inspiration created an internal motivation powerful enough to produce action, and more important, a lasting change in my little-kid

GO BIG TIP

If you want to create lasting momentum, focus on inspiration, not persuasion.

life. I instantly saw myself as a Lost Boy, and I took Toys"R"Us action to make sure I'd be the best Lost Boy I could be.

One of your main goals as an organization—as a brand—should be to inspire others to identify themselves with you, to inspire others toward action and community. If you can inspire them, you'll give them the internal motivation necessary to mobilize and fight alongside your organization. That's essentially what has happened in the trick shot community. There's an incredible amount of momentum there, and it's humbling to know that we play a role in inspiring more and more people to come on board.

I say it's humbling; let me explain that. The main reason it's humbling isn't because we have an opportunity to tell others how to make their basketball videos cooler. We enjoy doing that, but that isn't what gets to us. What blows us away is that we have an opportunity to speak into the lives of viewers who look up to us, to encourage and inspire them to pursue their dreams, to make a significant impact on their lives. The reason it's humbling is because as we read e-mails and watch videos from Indiana, California, New Jersey, Germany, New Zealand, the United Kingdom, Australia, Saudi Arabia, and almost every other place you can think of, we think about the kids, teenagers, and adults on the other end of the Internet, and we realize just how big our potential for influence really is.

Seeing our influence potential grow is incredibly motivating. And for you—as you'll hear more about in the next section—no matter what your Go Big dream is, as you continue to build your brand, you'll see your platform and influence potential grow as well.

In our opinion, having the opportunity to influence someone, especially someone younger than you, is a privilege. Having been kids ourselves, we know there's only enough space for a certain number of influencers in a child's life. If Dude Perfect can be one of those influencers, we are honored, and we take that role seriously.

Our desire to influence, impact, and inspire others is the reason I wrote this book. It's the reason we've made our Go Big mind-set such a public thing. By sharing our Go Big mind-set, my hope is to inspire others—yes, by the way we *view* life, but also by the way we live it. Inspiring others means broadening their viewpoint, pointing them toward something they didn't necessarily see before or refocusing them on something they once loved. To inspire people is to raise their eyes above and beyond what they currently see. It's purposefully pointing their view toward something of value, something worth pursuing. Inspiring others means seeing in them the potential they don't see in themselves . . . and then telling them that. It's bringing out the best in the people you reach.

Do this: as you continue to pursue your Go Big dream, make sure your organization intentionally *aims* at inspiration. There are lots of ways to do this, but we'll suggest a few.

First, identify and elevate your organization's overarching goal—the main reason your dream exists in the first place. Chances are, your team believes strongly in what you are doing. Capitalize on that passion by continually reminding your team members what it is you're all striving for—the significance of what you do. In bringing to light the overarching meaning of your organization, you take the focus off the minutiae of the process and inspire your team to remember the importance of the goal. It's internal versus external motivation. Don't get me

GO BIG TIP

To inspire people is to raise their eyes above and beyond what they currently see.

WRITING THIS BOOK

I wrote this book because I wanted to inspire others to pursue their own Go Big dreams. What's cool is that doing so has been a Go Big journey of my own. This book is my real-life application of the Go Big process we've been talking about. It's further proof that what we've been saying is for real.

wrong—keep your employee-of-the-month program. Just make sure you realize that an incentivized team member isn't as effective in the long run as someone passionately focused on the purpose of your organization.

Next, intentionally affirm each of your team members' roles in your organization. In our experience, the times each of us felt most engaged and excited within Dude Perfect have been when we felt most needed and appreciated by the rest of the team. If you truly want to inspire your team members, point out the potential you see in them and remind them that their roles truly matter.

Finally, promote fun in the workplace. Because you are all pursuing a Go Big dream, I already know your team members enjoy what they do. However, raising the atmosphere of your work environment from pleasant to fun should be one of your organization's top priorities. There is almost nothing more inspirational or motivational than allowing your team members every reason to smile during their jobs.

I love this truth. In fact, two of my favorite quotes involve this idea. The first is a statement by Dale Carnegie, the author behind the classic bestselling book *How to Win Friends and Influence People*. Carnegie states, "People rarely succeed at anything unless they have fun doing it." I couldn't agree more. The second and slightly less profound quote is from Buddy the Elf, played by Will Ferrell in the movie *Elf*. Buddy, arguably the wisest elf of all time, informs his new boss, "Smiling is my favorite." Buddy's emphasis on fun, while clearly a joke in the movie, is a great goal for all of us to aim for. In fact, because the guys and I refer to ourselves as "The Ambassadors of Fun," we've come to embrace Buddy's statement as one of our mottoes. It sounds a little crazy, but trust us, if you want to inspire those you work with, make sure to prioritize fun.

At the end of the day, you've got two options: achieve temporary results by persuading others, or focus on inspiring others and create lasting momentum, positively impacting those you reach. Choose the second option. It does take effort, but as you'll soon see, the results far outweigh the work.

To that point, I want to end this section with a message we recently received from a family that watches our videos on YouTube. Much to our delight, this family informed us, "When asked what he wants to be when he grows up, our three-year-old says, 'a Dude Perfect guy.'"

PART FIVE

GIVE BACK

CHAPTER 18
THE RED CARPET

We were picked up from the airport (in a GMC, of course) and dropped off at our hotel in downtown Los Angeles. The hotel was nice—we're talking rooftop-pool, hotel-branded-slippers type of nice. After taking some rooftop skyscraper pictures in the early evening, the guys and I and Mr. T strolled over to a cool restaurant in the heart of downtown LA.

We'd been to Los Angeles before, but never this close to the Nokia Theatre. Outside, the event staff was already setting up—lights, huge stages, barriers on all sides. This was an extravagant, high-production event. And if it was that showy on the outside, we were guessing the inside must have been out of control. With good food, great rest, and perfect weather, we were ready for the next day's main event.

At about 5:00 p.m.—an hour before showtime—I walked toward Ty's room, the spot we'd chosen as our meeting place. When I went inside, I realized all the guys were staring me down—but not in a "you're in trouble" way. No, it was an "I'm

TRICK SHOOTING 101

If someone puts you up in a nice hotel, walk around by the pool. You may be able to invite an NBA free agent to play for your city's basketball team.

looking at your clothes" kind of way. I'd seen girls do that to each other all the time—looking the other one up and down, straight-up judging her for what she was wearing—but this was definitely a first for me. Then, out of nowhere, I felt myself doing the same thing. I glanced at what each of the guys was wearing, made mental notes in my head about it, and finally, like coming out of a trance, I was free again.

There are only a few occasions when a guy is allowed to judge—or even care—what his friends are wearing:

1. He's in a wedding.
2. He's meeting the president.
3. He's attending the ESPYs—*scratch that*—walking the red carpet at the ESPYs.

There's the Grammys for music, the Oscars for movies, and then there's the ultimate sports-based awards show, the ESPYs, hosted by ESPN, "The Worldwide Leader in Sports." Because of our recent involvement with GMC, one of the event's lead sponsors, we were asked to attend the ESPYs. By itself, that would have been great—we couldn't have asked for anything cooler—but on top of that, they asked if we'd do an interview about our GMC campaign . . . on the red carpet.

In case you're keeping score, asking if we wanted to come to the ESPYs definitely qualifies as a dumb question. Of course we wanted to! We're some of the biggest sports fans on the planet, and this is one of the premier sports events. And the red carpet? We didn't even know how to wrap our minds around that part. All I could think was, *Let me pray about it. . . . Yes.*

And *that* is why we inspected what each of us was wearing.

Standing in that hotel room, we graded each other's red carpet looks:

- Dressy jeans and boots—reppin' Texas.
- Super classy dress shirts—sport coats on top.
- Stunner shade sunglasses—for outside *and* inside.
- Shirts untucked and skinny ties hanging loose—the *I don't care, but really I do* look.
- Coby's all-white, logo-shining Nike belt.
- Ty's bling-bling watch—thanks to his granddad's killer JCPenney associate discount.

Preparing our red carpet looks gave us a tiny glimpse into why Lady Gaga and others often dress so crazy. Red carpets give you this weird, almost compulsive need to choose something *more* than normal—it's a green light for fashion, or at least it feels that way. Walking out of our hotel all snazzied up, we felt pretty good about our collective look. Not that it mattered. This was our first rodeo, and no matter what we wore, we were about to be seriously shown up.

Talking to our driver on the way over, we learned that you *can* buy tickets to the ESPYs. You can attend the event and watch the awards. You can take pictures and hope you're sitting next to a famous person in the auditorium. And no doubt, all of that is extremely cool. What was significantly cooler, however, were the red carpet tickets in our pockets—the ones you *can't* buy.

We rolled up to the scene, halfway expecting to step into a mob of paparazzi snapping pictures of us because they have to, not because they know who we are. But while that type of high-profile entrance might exist somewhere else, it's not like that at the ESPYs. We opened the door not to paparazzi, but to serious-faced security. They took a look at our red carpet tickets, made sure they weren't counterfeit, and pointed us toward the security tent. Once inside, we were scanned and swept and beeped and x-rayed and eventually cleared for red carpet take-off. On the other side of the door, we could hear a crowd cheer as names were announced. Now it was showtime.

The door slowly opened, and as the bright light poured over us, the booming loudspeaker announced, "Please join me in welcoming to the ESPYs the Internet sensation, the premier trick basketball shooting entertainers, Dude Perfect!"

We were only a few paces in now, and an ESPN badge–wearing man ushered us to the left of the carpet and into the on deck section, where entrants with a scheduled interview would wait. From this position, I could see everything more clearly. To the right, running the length of the carpet and shielded by a low-lying velvet-rope barrier, stood a temporary grand-stand—elevated bleachers where the crowd could look down on the various personalities as they entered the venue. And to the left, the side we were on, were media stations—sectioned off squares of carpet where assorted television and radio personalities conducted ongoing, live interviews with the constant flow of high-profile ESPY attendees.

Turning our attention back to the task at hand, we looked to our left, to the live interview spot we'd occupy next. Moments from now, live on ESPN, we'd be interviewed by the celebrated sports reporter Erin Andrews. And for everyone who knows who that is, yes, she's extremely pretty. Yes, I was excited to meet her. And yes, a picture of us standing together was my Facebook profile picture for at least a month. I don't know what else to say, except that she likes me. And yes, that's official—remember, this isn't a tabloid; it's a book.

As for the interview, it went great. Our job was to highlight our involvement in the GMC campaign, and that's exactly what we did. Fielding questions from Erin, Tyler did a great job of conveying the message we were *supposed* to say as well as the Dude Perfect values we always strive to include.

After he said a few things about the campaign, Tyler ended by stating, "We feel really blessed to have this opportunity."

We've talked a little about this idea already, but the way we see it, there are two types of speech-givers: entitled ones and grateful ones. The entitled person says, "I deserve this." The grateful person, on the other hand, acknowledges that others have helped him or her succeed. In our case, we know that God has played an undeniable role in our story. Because of that, we often use interviews as opportunities to give him the credit he deserves. We make an effort to say that because we want others to know who we really are—five guys who love God and want to use the platform he's given us in order to help others.

Whether it's a live interview or a personal congratulation from a friend, we admit that moments in the spotlight are great, and when you're striving to be the best, recognition comes with the territory. But remember, the way you handle yourself in those spotlight moments says a lot about your organization and about you as an individual.

So how are you going to act? What are you going to say? Do you believe that you completely *earned* the platform you have? Or do you agree with us, that whether you deserve it or not, the platform you have is a gift—an opportunity? Do you believe

TRICK SHOOTING 101

When approaching famous people, send the tallest guy in your group. That way, celebrities might mistake you for someone important.

your responsibility is to use that platform for a purpose other than yourself, a purpose greater than yourself?

It's important to answer these questions. Your responses will guide your everyday actions, and then when spotlight moments come your way, you'll know where you stand. We've decided that if we're ever in a position to accept praise, we'll try to do so with a grateful attitude. That's the way we genuinely feel, so that's what we want to reflect to the public eye—in our interviews, on our website, everywhere we appear.

Pleased with our interview, we chatted with Erin for a few more minutes, took a picture for Facebook, and stepped back down toward the red runway. We'd just taken our first famous-person picture—good timing, because we needed a warm-up.

We think pictures are a million times cooler than autographs. An autograph says, "This famous person was here"— unless it's fake, which is a whole other story. A picture of you *with* a famous person says, "We were here together." Boom. Undeniable proof. And the best part, when you're in a picture with someone else, you look like you're best friends, and everyone wants to be best friends with famous people.

So how many Sharpies did we bring? Exactly zero. We were serious: we didn't want any autographs. Instead, we brought a camera, and we planned to use it. And as we sauntered down the red carpet, it was finally time to unleash the picture plan.

This probably goes without saying, but I'll say it anyway: famous people are tall—especially famous athletes. You know, like the ones who go to the ESPYs? Fortunately for us, we had our very own tall, famous-looking Dude Perfect member with us. Famous ESPYs people, meet Cody Jones.

Six foot six, super outgoing, tall, dark, and handsome

THE TALL FACTOR

This strategy worked so well that we used it for the rest of the night. Later, Cody claimed to have been nervous, but he sure didn't look like it. After each of our surprise camera-swarming appearances, we had a blast talking to the athletes. Almost every one of them was as down to earth as we are—just taller.

enough, Cody turned out to be an incredible ESPYs wingman. Here's why.

After we walked a ways, we slid to our right, picked a spot, and camped out on the red carpet. In that position we waited until one of us spotted someone we wanted to meet, someone we wanted to take a picture with. At that point, we'd send Cody. Doing what we physically couldn't, Cody walked up to an athlete—Jason Witten, for example—confidently looked him in the eye, shook his hand, and said something along the lines of, "Hey, Jason, my name is Cody Jones. I'm here with a group called Dude Perfect, some of the guys who do those crazy basketball shots."

At this point, we'd occasionally hear a big, smiling "No way!" from an athlete who happened to know about our stuff. And every time it happened, it felt crazy. Athletes from all across the country, and even the world, knew about our videos, often down to the names of the shots. One athlete said, "The laser shot is by far my favorite."

But whether they knew about us or not, Cody would proceed the same way. "Well, hey, I don't want to keep you, but I was wondering if I could get a quick picture?"

Super cool about it, they'd say yes, setting us up for our favorite part. As soon as Cody and the famous person posed for a picture, the rest of us would quickly, almost in a blur, surround the duo, throw our arms around each of them, face the camera, and smile. Understandably, as we bookended them, we got some priceless reactions from confused athletes. Usually they quickly realized, *Oh, this is the rest of your group*, but we're convinced some of them thought that several random guys had made it into their picture.

Here is the last thing I'll say about our time on the red carpet. For two years now, we'd seen various ESPN television and radio show hosts talk about us, but unfortunately, we hadn't met them. Then, as we approached the end of the carpet, standing on the left side—the media side—were show host after show host, people we loved, people we'd only been able to thank by e-mail so far. Thrilled by the opportunity to show our appreciation in person, we shared enthusiastic hugs and handshakes with everyone we could find. We hung out with Colin Cowherd and Michelle Beadle, for example, the hosts of *SportsNation*—the show that's aired our stuff probably more than any other. And we would have accidentally slipped by Mike and Mike, ESPN's epic radio hosts, if Mike Golic hadn't recognized us and flagged us down. As we met and thanked so many of the folks who had helped us over the past two years, it made us realize, yet again, just how many people had played a role in our getting to that carpet.

As you think about your Go Big journey, we'd encourage you to consider how you might thank those who have helped you get where you are. And since others have given their time and effort in assisting you, think about what you could give them in return. We've found that, when it comes to a thank-you gift, it's not about the money you spend. Regardless of what you give, what you're really doing is packaging your appreciation and giving it to someone who clearly deserves it. You're taking some of your time and effort and spending it on someone who has already poured into your life. That's worth your time every time.

As we expected, the actual awards show was unbelievable. The Nokia Theatre was breathtaking. The size, the setup, the tricked-out stage—everything was impressive. Enormous video screens drew our attention to every corner. The musicians and the acoustics—phenomenal. We felt every single drumbeat, every single high note.

On top of that, GMC had hooked us up. Our seats were about fifteen rows from the stage. There were famous people everywhere we looked, all around us—many sitting farther back than we were. The entertainers and comedians were awesome, especially Will Ferrell, one of our favorites. His vuvuzela routine will undoubtedly go down in ESPY history.

After every ESPY award had been handed out, after the show had ended and people were making their way out of the building, security let people come up on the stage. Taking advantage of this final opportunity, we made our way up the stairs, turned around to face the now-empty auditorium, and in that moment, squinting in the lights, confetti showering down around us, like thousands of stars had done, I stared out and up at the massive auditorium. It was quite a sight, one I won't soon forget.

But for a few moments, standing where I stood, my mind drifted somewhere else—somewhere I didn't tell it to go. While it would have made sense to think about the past couple of years' confetti-covered *American Idol* winners, that's not what happened. For just a minute, staring deep into the lights, I thought about our backyard. I thought about a group of guys throwing basketballs over their heads, behind their backs, and off a roof—and filming it, just for fun. I thought about the last two years, all the e-mails, phone calls, shots, and videos—all the hard work we'd put in. I thought about our rocket-propelled story, how one thing led to another, and how even when it got tough, we never gave up. I thought about all the people who had helped us along the way—especially Mr. T and the impact

ON THE RED CARPET

Here are some of the people we met at the ESPYs: Tim Tebow, Colt McCoy, Dr. J, Terrell Owens, Landon Donovan and the USA men's soccer team, Jay Williams, Stuart Scott, Mark Ingram Jr., Chris Johnson, Jason Witten, Wade Phillips, Chris Berman, and Georges St-Pierre.

he'd made on our lives. Finally, I thought about the words *Go Big*, our slogan. And as I considered the phrase, I realized that no matter how big our imagination, no matter how inspired our dream, we never could have imagined this. In that moment, I quietly thanked God for the past two years. His plan for us had been way bigger than any we could have come up with ourselves. In that moment, I felt more grateful than I can explain.

A lot of incredible things had happened that night—things great Facebook statuses and tweets are made of. For us, that night was a celebration of the dream we'd been chasing for a while. It was a public recognition that, at least to some degree, we'd really begun to reach our goals. But the moment I had as I stood onstage and reflected on our journey—*that's* what this chapter is really about.

With the pages we have left, we're going to look at the fifth and final Go Big principle, the last rung to the ladder, the action we believe should be the purpose for your dream in the first place: Give Back. We're going to explain how, with the unique platform you've been given, you have an opportunity, and in fact a responsibility, to leverage that platform to impact the lives of others.

The reason for the chapter you just read is simple. Before we went any further, before we dove into all that Give Back has to offer, we wanted to stress that in order to best give to others, you have to first realize what has been given to you. Thankfulness is the starting point. If you haven't already, we want you to move forward with a grateful attitude; it can go a long way, both on the microphone and in your Give Back actions. Giving back—not standing on a lit-up, confetti-filled stage—is by far the most fulfilling part of our journey so far.

GO BIG TIP

In order to best give to others, you have to first realize what has been given to you.

With every basketball-throwing, living-room-wrestling, lemon-eating bone in our bodies, we believe that God has given us our Dude Perfect platform for a cause much greater than ourselves. And as we're about to show you, there's nothing else like it.

with Michelle and Colin

with Dr. J

with Colt McCoy

with Erin Andrews

with Jason Witten

with Tim Tebow

CHAPTER 19
PERSONAL FOUL

Overall, we're pretty nice guys. A few things, however, can get us a little riled up. One is a cheap foul on the basketball court. Take one of our intramural games at Texas A&M, for example. It was the second half, and the atmosphere was heated. I got a steal, took it the length of the court, and as I went in for a layup, one of the opposing players swooped in behind me, took my legs out from under me, and I fell—hard. Now look, I've played ball my whole life, so I understand giving someone a good, solid foul. There's nothing wrong with the old-school *if you're gonna foul him, foul him hard* mentality. But there's a difference between sending someone a message and taking his legs out from under him. That's some dangerous stuff—and that's exactly what happened.

Like I said, I fell hard. It was one of those thuds that, just hearing it, stays with you, the kind that makes you wince. The moment I went down, both teams' crowds went silent. The players—well, not so much. For a moment, I couldn't really tell what was happening. Lying on the court, my ears were ringing from the impact. I opened my eyes, but everything looked blurry. I slowly rolled over onto my back. Sound muted and vision hazy, I could tell there was some "activity" on the court. As the cloudiness faded, I saw a husky shape—clearly Tyler—standing in the face of the player who had just taken me out. Even in that state, I remember thinking, *This is not gonna be good.*

By now you've probably realized that the guys and I treat each other like brothers. That means we get on each other's nerves, but it also means we're loyal, sometimes to a fault. So to the Dude Perfect guys on the court with me, that foul had just gotten real personal, real fast.

Ty was staring a hole through the smaller guy's eyes. The tension was incredible. I thought I was about to see the shortest fight of all time. Usually we're not fighters; that's just not how we handle stuff. But the other player didn't know that. I could tell he was trying to decide what to do, and as I slowly stood up, I couldn't pull my gaze away from the rapidly developing situation in front of me. I'd never seen Tyler hit a real person, but we have one of those martial arts "Big Bob" practice dummies at our house, and watching him whale on that thing had always caused a mixture of feelings somewhere between laughter and terror. Apparently liking his face the way it was, the kid slowly backed away.

Tyler, still fuming, turned his attention to the referee. Looking at the striped peacekeeper, Ty said what soon became a memorable quote for us: "Look, if that happens again, we're gonna have a serious problem."

Like I said, we don't get too upset about a whole lot of

INTRAMURAL BASKETBALL

Like the rest of us, Tyler gets down to business when it comes to intramural basketball. During one of our games, I was able to catch this conversation:

Opposing team's player: "Dang, man. Y'all are killing us."

Tyler: "Yep."

"Any advice?"

"Yeah, don't stop hustling."

"That's hard."

"Okay, well, you're gonna lose."

things, but similar to a cheap foul against one of our friends, there's another thing that bothers us a lot—so much so that we focused our fifth and last principle on it.

There's just one more piece to the puzzle, one more crucial idea that you have to grab hold of if you want to represent and experience all that makes up the Go Big mind-set. All the principles we've talked about are important, but this last one is nonnegotiable. It's *this* one that, if you refuse to adopt it, we'll probably take it personally. Yes, we believe that ignoring this fifth and final principle—Give Back—is a deal breaker. So as much as we want you hanging out in the clubhouse with us, this last thing is the secret password you'll need in order to enter. If you don't care, fine. Enjoy someone else's club. But if you want to join ours, you've got to give back.

Pause. Read that again: *give back.*

Now if I had to guess the word you're currently thinking about, the word that comes to mind when you see the phrase "Give Back," I'd guess it's *charity.* That's because when most people think about giving time and money, *charity* seems like the best term. Well, whether *charity* or some other word came to your mind, whether positive or negative thoughts rose to the surface, take the knee-jerk reaction you just had to that Give Back phrase and completely ignore it.

I'm about to explain why we get upset, but before I do, I want to define the Give Back principle as just that—a principle, nothing more, nothing less. What you choose to do with that principle is up to you. Just know that our opinion of you rides heavily on that decision.

A principle is a pretty cool thing. It's a truth that, if adopted, acts as a filter for future actions. Take Blink Later, for example.

Anytime the guys and I face a decision that involves the fast-paced, connected world, we run it through the Blink Later filter. And if we base our actions on the truth of that principle, we know we can move forward with confidence. Basically, when it comes to the connected world, we have chosen to have a Blink Later mind-set. In the same way, that's what we mean when we talk about our Go Big mind-set. Our five principles mesh together to form a collective grid that helps us make good decisions.

So now, with that in mind, let's look at Give Back. In our opinion, having a Give Back mind-set isn't about charity; it's about having an others-centered perspective. See, a charity mind-set says, "I have something generic to offer—usually money—so here you go. Use it, and help me look good and feel better." A Give Back mind-set is completely different. Why? There's absolutely nothing generic about it. Your unique Go Big dream has given you a unique platform. And having that unique platform means you can reach people no one else can and help them in ways no one else can. Because of the unique passions, connections, and skills your organization brings to the table, you can help others in ways that only you could even think of.

Since that's the case, we think your Give Back focus is more than just a cool opportunity; we think it's your *responsibility*. Because you're the only one who can help certain people in certain ways, you have a responsibility to use your platform to help those in your unique circle of influence. That, we believe, is a cause worth chasing—a cause much greater than yourself. And when people ignore or refuse that responsibility, *that* is what gets us riled up. Don't be the person who is so wrapped

GO BIG TIP

Having a Give Back mind-set isn't about charity; it's about having an others-centered perspective.

up in your own story that you fail in your responsibility to help those around you. That's not cool at all.

Here's the good news. If you're up for it, giving back can be more than something you occasionally do at the end of the year. Believe it or not, it can be something you're actually excited about. The key, we've found, is *you*. In the same way you build a Go Big dream around a passion, you can build your giving around something that stirs your heart.

Here's an example. After spending some time in Argentina, Blake Mycoskie was impacted by the reality that countless Argentinean children have no shoes to protect their feet. He learned that because these children lack footwear, they are highly susceptible to soil-transferred disease, as well as cut-induced infections. On top of that, because of dress-code regulations, these shoeless children are prevented from going to school.

After being faced with this reality, Blake easily could have done nothing—but he didn't. Blake came up with a brilliant dream: a one-for-one deal. He realized he could launch a business that manufactured simple shoes, and for every pair purchased in the United States, he could give one to a child in need. Blake's passion-based dream, a simple idea born out of a desire to bring aid to needy children, became TOMS Shoes.

Like TOMS, sometimes an organization's giving focus will match their organization's overall focus, but that's not always the case. Let me explain by showing you how both those scenarios play out in Dude Perfect World.

First, you might assume that we give back in a way that involves basketball, or at least sports—and, well, you'd be right. Like we've said a thousand times, we love competition. We eat it for breakfast. It fuels our love for sports, and it's one of the main reasons we love crazy basketball shots: we love to compete with each other, and we love the adrenaline of competing against ourselves. We also enjoy hanging out with competitive kids, kids who want to go big—whether they know it yet or not. So with those passions in mind, we've tried to put our Give Back mind-set into action.

Something we're almost always up for doing, for example, is playing dodgeball. Dodgeball fund-raisers happen all the time, and when we hear of a cause we want to support, we support it on the court. Anytime giving back means hitting somebody with a dodgeball, sign me up.

TRICK SHOOTING 101

If you need a prize for a trick-shooting competition, a spray-painted water-melon is not the route to go. You'll taste a lot more paint and a lot less melon.

We also speak often at Fellowship of Christian Athletes groups. Whether it's a middle school or high school crowd, these sports-focused groups are a natural fit for us. We speak to the kids about pursuing their sports dreams, and we shoot around with them on the court. It's awesome.

In addition, we have the opportunity to visit hospitals and encourage kids who, for whatever reason, aren't able to play outside. By setting up a miniature basketball goal, we can give a child the chance to experience fun and competition—even in a hospital bed.

But not everything we do is based on sports or competition. One of our favorite Give Back focuses has been meeting some of the needs of children in Africa. Each of our families, as we grew up, supported a child through Compassion International, a Christian organization that helps lift children out of poverty all across the world. As Dude Perfect discussed ways we could give back, we couldn't run away from the fact that each of us wanted to support a child in Africa through this organization. So early on in our Go Big process, with the launch of our Summer Camp

Edition video, we began to publicly support some children in Africa through Compassion International. Our hope was that these actions would help the kids we personally supported, as well as encourage other people to get involved.

As I write this, I can't help but smile about another opportunity on the horizon. In the summer of 2011, a couple of the Dude Perfect guys are going on a mission trip to Africa. Expanding on our passion for the children of this continent, we are partnering with two other organizations to personally, physically make an impact on the other side of the world. We'll oversee the finishing stages of a well that will bring clean water to thousands of people who desperately need it. We'll visit orphanages, spending time with children who receive very little personal attention or love, especially from positive male role models.

That trip would be great by itself, but we've identified a unique way we can help. The particular children we'll be visiting already have their essential needs met. They have food, water, and shelter. And since Visiting Orphans, the organization we're going with, specializes in giving individual care, love, and attention to the children, we realized there was another aspect that could be missing in these children's lives: fun. Now that may sound dumb, but ask any kid around how important fun is to them. It's a huge deal, and as it turns out, we're kind of professionals at having and bringing fun. Like I said earlier, one of the titles we've adopted throughout this two-year journey is "The Ambassadors of Fun."

Taking our title across the globe, we've partnered with Spalding and Nerf, two companies we work with, to supply the orphanages we visit with toys and sporting equipment. From

OUR AFRICA TRIP

See what happened on our Africa trip by visiting our website.

DudePerfect.com

what we understand, for the first time in their lives, these kids will be able to own something fun. You're right, we won't be saving those particular children's lives—that's already happened because of the help of the various organizations involved. But we will be bringing joy to the lives of thousands of children, children just like the ones you and I have in our lives—our brothers, sisters, cousins, nieces, nephews—children with names and faces and tears and smiles. As "The Ambassadors of Fun," we can give back from a unique specialty of ours. By the time you read this, we'll be back from the African plains. I can't wait to tell you about the experiences we have there.

Sports, dodgeball, competition, Africa—for us, there's an x-factor in almost all of the Give Back focuses we've chosen. The biggest part of each of our lives, the passion we want to reflect most in our Give Back actions, is our personal relationship with Jesus Christ. Our faith plays a large role in who we are as individuals and who Dude Perfect is as a group. That's why, when we visit children in the hospital, we ask if we can pray for them. It's also the reason we support groups like Compassion International that help some of the neediest children on the planet in the name of Jesus.

Some people think we do this Give Back stuff so we'll get brownie points with God—false. The reason we help others is because we want to share God's love with people who might not know him. Jesus changed each of our lives for the better, and we want others to experience the joy that we have. Look, we promise to never preach at you. We don't like that any more than the next guy. But if you ever have questions about God, shoot us an e-mail. We always have time to talk about the God who changed our lives.

COMPASSION INTERNATIONAL

Check out Compassion International, one of the organizations we partner with. They do great work, and we love supporting them.

compassion.com

Whether you believe in Jesus or not, the truth is that you and I both have a unique opportunity to use the stages we've been given to impact those around us. What you need to decide is this: What uniquely stirs you from a Give Back perspective? Which of your passions do you want to explore for ways you can uniquely help others? Like the dodgeball tournaments, some of your answers will be ideas that already exist. With those, all you have to do is join in with what others are already doing. And other answers, like the Africa trip, are brand-new and need to be molded to the shape of what you uniquely have to offer. We're "The Ambassadors of Fun." What's your specialty?

The way I see it, you and I have an opportunity, and in fact a responsibility, to look outside ourselves and use our unique platforms to help those around us. We have a chance to make a Go Big impression on the world. Let's not be the type of people who make it all about us. No one likes that guy. Instead, let's give thanks to God and give back to others.

We've seen the impact that giving back can have on *us*. When someone chooses not to give back, they miss out on that experience. They miss out on the Go Big opportunity to help others and broaden their own Go Big view of the world. To be honest, we're not worried about any of you. We believe that with a truly Go Big perspective, you'll allow your unique passions to drive you to help others in ways no one else can. Trust us; it's worth it. Every time we've taken the initiative to give back, we've found that our Go Big lens, the one we see the world through, expands significantly. And that's always a good thing. Try it and you'll see. Giving back is addicting.

GO BIG TIP

Because of the uniqueness of your platform, you can reach and help groups of people that no one else can.

CHAPTER 20
GO BIG

There's an undeniable fascination with taking normal achievements to the limit. Children try to run before they walk. Women join advanced yoga classes, their husbands advanced basketball leagues—both before they're ready. We go from JV to varsity, bachelor's degrees to master's, and master's to doctorates. We ski tougher slopes, play harder songs, lift heavier weights, get better jobs, fly to higher heights, run longer distances, and choose to have at least one more child who will, of course, try running before walking.

But that's not enough, so at night, we dream. Right now, for example, kids around the globe are dreaming about sports. If we could get inside their heads, I doubt we'd see too many first downs, singles, assists, or layups. But I'd bet all the money in the world that touchdowns, home runs, hat tricks, buzzer beaters, and high-flying dunks surround their visions of glory. How do I know this? The same way you do: neither of us ever dreamed within that first list. But there's a much more convincing reason, one you've probably heard countless times, and it displays this idea better than I ever could:

"Duh nuh nuh, duh nuh nuh . . . Thisss is SportsCenter."

It's tough to explain, but when SportsCenter's Top Ten Plays comes on, most guys pause their lives, not their televisions. Things that mattered a lot matter a lot less for about two minutes. The ten most inspirational, head-shaking, are-you-kidding-me plays of the day—*that's* what kids dream about.

Clearly there's an intangible pride and sense of accomplishment associated with going big, and I think that's awesome. I believe we're all wired that way. I know Dude Perfect is for sure.

THE SNOWMAN

We built the biggest snowman College Station had ever seen. It quickly became known as "The Snowman."

Here's an example. When it snowed at Texas A&M, it was a huge deal. Snow is cold and Texas is hot, so trust me, it was a *stop studying, there's something falling out of the sky* big deal. A few sled rides and snowball fights later, we hopped in the car and drove through town. As we passed house after house, we noticed there were lots of snowmen in people's yards, but they were all the same size—small. As you undoubtedly know by now, Dude Perfect doesn't exactly do *small*. So that night, with a few other friends, we went to the campus golf course and built the biggest snowman College Station has ever seen.

Here's the deal: everyone loves the idea of going big. But not everyone acts on it.

Plenty of fun memories and carrot-nosed snowmen were formed that day, and each one was definitely worth building. You and I both know that making less of a snowman doesn't make you less of a person, but here's the point: Sometimes we have grand visions, dreams of truly epic proportion, but instead of acting on those, instead of taking practical steps to move toward them, we let the pressures we face, the insecurities in our minds, and the busyness of our lives drown out the things that can make our hearts beat the way they were designed.

I'm not saying it's easy. Building that snowman was horrible; ask any of us who helped. But even though it took me two hours to feel my hands again, you know what happened? Tyler and I, along with the other helpers there, saw countless Go Big glimmers in the eyes of the people who came to take pictures with what quickly became known as "The Snowman."

That day in the snow, our Go Big mind-set had a nose and a huge crowd of people around him. Only a couple of blocks away, in our backyard, that mind-set had changed our lives.

I've given it my absolute best, from backyard to red carpet, but these pages could never do justice to the Go Big journey we've been on—or the one that's waiting for you. Our sincere desire is that through the Go Big mind-set, you will pursue your dreams. So explore your passions—choose a dream that you instinctively *get excited* about. With that dream in your sights, *own it*; fully embrace and relentlessly pursue your vision. And as you do, as you chase down your dream, don't get caught standing still: act now—*blink later*. Along the way, *inspire others*—it's the best way to create and sustain lasting momentum. Finally, *give back*; use the platform you've been given for a purpose greater than yourself.

I wrote this book because we at Dude Perfect want others to see the world differently than they did before. We want you to look at your life through a Go Big lens. Take it from us—it *will* change your life.

When we hear someone on TV say that Dude Perfect really "goes big," that's one of the best compliments we can receive. Creating that perception is a goal for us because, like building The Snowman, we know that going big can be inspirational for others. Every once in a while, however, someone labels us as *successful*. Now some people, those who don't read this book, might assume that *success* and *going big* mean the same thing. Because of that, they might assume that our being labeled "successful" would be encouraging. And while they'd be right to some degree, the truth is that raw success isn't really our goal.

Just turn on the television, and you'll see that every day someone achieves personal success or international fame. The problem is that far too often these successful people choose to waste their opportunities, their platforms, and the unique leverage they've been given. That's where a Go Big person rises above the crowd. Going big doesn't mean gaining an audience or a platform for your own personal glory. We believe there's more to it than that.

The guys and I believe that going big means realizing that the God who gave us this platform wants us to use it for his glory. If that sounds weird to you, I understand, but stay with me. I once heard Craig Groeschel speak at a leadership conference. He said to a room filled with Go Big people, "Your glory is too small a thing to live for." I thought about that phrase for a long time. *My glory is too small a thing to live for?* Often our personal glory feels like a pretty big thing—sometimes the *only* thing. But if chasing our own glory was really that worthwhile, then why do we get a sick feeling in our stomachs and a twisted look on our faces when we hear champion athletes or Academy Award winners say how great they are, how much they deserve that award, and how proud they are of themselves? It happens all the time, and it always sounds ridiculous.

By speaking highly of themselves, they taint their accomplishments; what was once worth praising is quickly washed out by self-admiration. We believe there's a better way to go big. When others see our videos online, hear us talk on television, or read this book, we want them to see us bringing and giving glory to God. Like I said in the last chapter, that's one of the main reasons we work with deserving charities and nonprofit organizations. It's not to get more exposure, and we couldn't care less if you think we're simply good guys. We do it because God has given us a platform, and we want to leverage it to help others.

If you haven't already noticed, we mention God a lot, maybe more than you'd like to hear. But as I've already promised, we're not going to preach at you. Here's how we handle the subject of God, and more specifically, Jesus Christ. While we never tell people what to believe, we often tell people what *we* believe. People ask us in interviews all the time, for example, about the "God stuff" they see on our website. We simply tell them that Jesus Christ changed each of our lives for the better, and because of that, our relationship with him is very important to us—as individuals and as a group.

In our experience, nothing has been able to fulfill us except for Jesus Christ: not academic success, not state basketball championships, not money, not beautiful girlfriends. We all became Christians before Dude Perfect was born, but looking back, even the taste of fame we've experienced does not begin

GO BIG TIP

Our own personal glory is far too small a thing to live for.

to compare with the joy of having Jesus fill the emptiness in our lives.

Going big is awesome. It's an instinctive desire, and you should run hard in that pursuit. But we believe that going big without figuring out God's part just won't be enough. Even going big and handling the platform right, giving to kids overseas and helping others, won't be truly fulfilling without a personal relationship with God. The Bible says that God has "set eternity in the human heart" (Ecclesiastes 3:11). We believe that God put the idea of epic perfection inside of us. That's why people who don't know God constantly strive for more, reach it, and still feel empty. It's a confusing cycle, and it's not fun.

Three years ago, none of us would have thought we'd be where we are now. We all had our own separate plans, and to us, they felt huge. But God said no to some of our plans. He stepped in and authored for us a very different adventure. But from where we're standing now, we'd all agree that his plans for us have been way bigger than any we could have thought of ourselves. If the whole Jesus thing makes no sense to you, if it sounds like a crutch for the weak or a prescription for missing out on what life has to offer, we promise you that's the farthest thing from the truth. The Bible says that Jesus came to bring you life, and life to the fullest (see John 10:10).

We're not saying God makes everything perfect or easy—that certainly hasn't been the case for us. But following God's Go Big plan for our lives has certainly been worthwhile. The truth is, even though living by God's design is difficult, God has filled us with a peace that, at the end of the day, even in the midst of our struggles and missed shots, is the reason we smile.

If you're curious about God, just talk to him, or talk to

GO BIG TIP

God put the idea of epic perfection inside of us. That's why people who don't know God constantly strive for more, reach it, and still feel empty.

someone about him—you can even talk to us. We'd love to tell you more. So why am I saying this? Do I think I'll sell more books by talking about God? Exactly the opposite. The reason I want to say this is because we believe it. Jesus is the most important part of our story, and he is the one who has enabled us to go big.

I'm not ending this book by talking about God because I want to trick you into hearing what we think about Jesus. That's not a secret. It's all over our website, and the media scooped that story a long time ago. I've chosen to end *Go Big* with a conversation about God because every Dude Perfect member believes that God is the inventor of big, the inventor of you and me, and the inventor of each of our Go Big dreams. And when all is said and done, when all our shots are over and our equipment is put away, he is the one who deserves the spotlight.

ACKNOWLEDGMENTS

In chapter 3, I mentioned that tons of people have helped us during this crazy journey. As you look at this list, you'll see more clearly what we've come to know beyond a doubt: you can't go big on your own, and there's no reason to try.

We would like to thank:

First and most important . . . our Lord and Savior, Jesus Christ.

Each and every Dude Perfect family member for putting up with our craziness:

- Coby and Cory's family: parents Larry and Diann; sister Catherine; Larry and Becky Hill; Steve and Sue Cotton and kids; grandparents Meme and Pop, Nana and Granddad
- Tyler's family: wife Bethany; parents Jeff and Pam; sister Paige; uncle Chris Cobb; uncle Don and aunt Becky; grandparents Neanie and Bob-Bob, Mema and Pa

- Special thanks to the ultimate work-doer: Jeff Toney, aka Mr. T, who, when he agreed to help us, had no idea what he was getting himself into. Thanks for being the greatest agent we could ever ask for . . . and for being a second dad to all of us.
- Cody's family: wife Allison; parents Steve and Jan; brothers Chase and Connor
- Garrett's family: wife Kristin; parents Jim and Cheryl; brothers Chase and Pierce
- Sean's family: wife Melanie; parents John and Sheila; brother Brian

The greatest roommates ever: Rusty, Cole, Travis, Calvin, and Carson.

The whole trick shot community for supporting us and constantly keeping us on our toes with your incredible videos! Y'all are the best!

Advice givers: Jimmy Hornbeak, Peter Strople, Reid Gettys, Kirk Novak, Anthony George, Mark Rae, Jack Stibbs, Chad Gauntt, Jay and Beth Nowlin, Jason and Maile Molin, Andrew and Boa Chen, Anne Long and Sarah Janosik, Warren Samuels, Jason Bankhead, Jim Zarbaugh, Tom Dyer, Charles Rutherford, Adam Donyes, and Joe White.

The Panda for being the greatest mascot and pal anyone could ever want.

Manic Bloom, the band responsible for the awesome music in most of our videos. Their upbeat sound has been with us since the beginning.

Television and publicity: Yahoo!, Jimmy Kimmel, *Inside Edition*, CBS's *The Early Show* and Harry Smith, CBS's Steve

Hartman, *Good Morning America*, *Fox & Friends*, CMT's *Country Fried Home Videos*, The Associated Press, KBTX's Shane McAuliffe, *The Dallas Morning News*, *Sports Illustrated*, and *LIVE! with Regis and Kelly*.

ESPN: The ESPYs award show, *Mike and Mike*, Colin Cowherd and Michelle Beadle of *SportsNation*, *Highlight Express*, Erin Andrews, *Pardon the Interruption*, *Around the Horn*, *1st and 10*, *First Take*, and *E:60*.

My literary agent and now close friend Roger Gibson. Thanks to Shay Robbins for introducing us.

Tyndale House Publishers: Ron Beers, Jon Farrar, Kara Leonino, Stephen Vosloo, Dean Renninger, April Kimura-Anderson, and everyone else involved in the humongous process. You all are the best!

Lead editor Jonathan Schindler. I've said it a million times, but it's still true. You the man.

Dude Perfect iPhone game: BlackBox Interactive, Big Bang Entertainment, Nick Glimcher, and Saban Burrell.

The greatest attorney ever, Sam Curphey. We can't thank you enough. Not only is your work excellent, but you are an absolute pleasure to work with.

Sky Ranch Summer Camp: John Morgan, staff, and all campers!

Prestonwood Baptist Church: Jim Wicker, Jack Graham, Scott Seal, Marc Rylander, Harvey Lecher, Chris Behm, Rick Briscoe, Chase Hilbert, and Corey Butler.

Video helpers: Connor Nichols, Luke Withers, Chase Hilbert, B. J. Holmes, Dash Harris, Austin Carey, Robert Rossman, Brandon Pender, and Bryan Jones.

Cory's high school teachers Mrs. Janet Abshire and

Mrs. Shannon Wiley for teaching me how to write. I could never do either of you justice!

Texas A&M University:

- Staff and teachers: President Lofton, Dr. Nancy Street, Dr. Joyce Juntune, and Dr. Jorge Vanegas
- Coach Mark Turgeon and the Texas A&M basketball team
- The Texas A&M hockey team
- *The Battalion* student newspaper
- Will King and The George Bush Presidential Library
- Mrs. Barbara Bush—the coolest First Lady of all time!
- Texas A&M's BYX and AMC for backing us the whole way.
- The Aggie Network for so strongly supporting us throughout this process.

Companies and organizations we have worked with: GMC, Spalding, Nerf, Southwest Airlines, AT&T, ESPN, Leo Burnett, Action Figure, Digg Communications, District Lines, Visiting Orphans, Compassion International, Catalyst Leadership Conference, and Fellowship of Christian Athletes.

Incredible YouTube Team: Julie Kikla, Andrew Bangs, and Matt Villacarte.

Original website designer, Disappearing Ink's Eric Foster.

Oscar Brown for designing our logo.

Our Sacramento family: Tyreke Evans, Tyreke's agent Phil Williams, Julius "Doc" and Reggie Evans, BluPrint, the whole Sacramento Kings organization, NBA legend and mayor of Sacramento Kevin Johnson, Kings VP Troy Hanson, and the Sacramento State Capitol Building staff.

Lupot's, Traditions, Inspirations, and Aggieland Outfitters for reppin' our merchandise!

The greatest neighbors of all time, Ken and Bobbie Denmark.

YouTube, Facebook, and Twitter for connecting us to the world.

LeBron James—seeing you enjoy one of our videos in person inspired me as much or more than any other event during this process. Special thanks to Daniel, Luke, Ashley, Rebekah, Omega, and Samantha for coming with me on that ridiculous adventure!

Rob Dyrdek for inspiring us to do cool things . . . and the impossible.

You know who you are: Ethan and Drew from the GMC shoot, Ricky McPherson, Jason Bolen, Rob Neal, Coach Mike Cooper, LaTroy Hawkins, Tori Hunter, USA soccer team, Jay Williams, our family at The Woodlands Apple Store, Chris Behm and the Dallas Cowboys, StoneBridge Church, SDSP and LTSP '09, The John Cooper School, Prosper High School, and Plano High School.

We want to sincerely thank every single person who has ever watched one of our videos.

Finally, we want to thank you for reading this book and being willing to go big with us. Your potential is the reason this book exists.

NOTES

CHAPTER 2: WHAT WE REALLY DO BEST

page 11   *Apple is the fastest-growing global brand:* Interbrand, "Best Global Brands: 2010 Rankings," http://www.interbrand.com/en/knowledge/best-global -brands/best-global-brands-2008/best-global-brands-2010.aspx.

CHAPTER 4: MEETING LEBRON

page 34   *no regard for human life:* This quote is from Kevin Harlan, the announcer at the Cavaliers/Celtics game where LeBron made this outrageous dunk. You can see the moment at http://www.youtube.com/watch?v =9MSQ_G5MZFo.

CHAPTER 8: THE SHOT SEEN 'ROUND THE WORLD

page 79   *Groupon expanded . . . to over 50 million:* Julie Mossler, "Groupon Raises, Like, a Billion Dollars" (Groupon press release), BusinessWire, January 10, 2011, http://www.businesswire.com/news/home/20110110006746/en /CORRECTING-REPLACING-Groupon-Raises-Billion-Dollars.

page 79   Forbes *magazine labeled Groupon the fastest-growing company ever:* Christopher Steiner, "Meet the Fastest Growing Company Ever," *Forbes,* August 30, 2010, http://www.forbes.com/forbes/2010/0830 /entrepreneurs-groupon-facebook-twitter-next-web-phenom.html.

CHAPTER 13: FULL SPEED AHEAD

page 124 Advertising Age *listed Dude Perfect . . . wanted to associate themselves with:* Irina Slutsky, "Meet YouTube's Most In-Demand Brand Stars," *Advertising Age,* September 13, 2010, http://adage.com/article/digital /meet-youtube-s-demand-brand-stars/145844.

page 129 *Coca-Cola gets almost everything right . . . with 11 million fans on Facebook and 96,385 followers on Twitter as of August 2010:* Interbrand, "Best Global Brands: 2010 Rankings," http://www.interbrand.com/en/best-global -brands/best-global-brands-2008/best-global-brands-2010.aspx.

CHAPTER 16: COOL THINGS

page 159 *People work better when they're involved in something they're passionate about:* Bharat Mediratta, as told to Julie Bick, "The Google Way: Give Engineers Room," *New York Times,* October 21, 2007, http://www.nytimes .com/2007/10/21/jobs/21pre.html?pagewanted=print.

CHAPTER 17: YOU MIGHT BE A TRICK SHOOTER IF . . .

page 168 *People rarely succeed at anything unless they have fun doing it:* Dale Carnegie, *How to Win Friends and Influence People* (New York: Simon & Schuster, 1981 [1936]), 71.

CHAPTER 18: THE RED CARPET

page 181 *His vuvuzela routine will undoubtedly go down in ESPY history:* You can check out his hilarious routine at http://www.youtube.com /watch?v=sDuBjUcLxaI.

YOU'VE SEEN THE VIDEOS.
YOU'VE READ THE BOOK.
NOW PLAY THE GAME.

 Search **"Dude Perfect"** in the App Store

Go Big with us:

.com/**DudePerfect**
.com/**DudePerfect**
.com/**DudePerfect**

To inquire about speaking engagements:
speaking@DudePerfect.com

www.DudePerfect.com